Yang Lian

杨炼

Also by Yang Lian

In English translation:

In Symmetry with Death
Masks and Crocodile
Non-Person Singular
Where the Sea Stands Still
Yi
Notes of a Blissful Ghost
Concentric Circles
Whaur the Deep Sea Devauls*
Unreal City

* *(translation into Scots)*

In Chinese:

礼魂
荒魂
黄
人的自觉
太阳与人
♀
鬼话
人景，鬼话
杨炼作品１９８２－１９９７
月蚀的七个半夜
杨炼作品１９８２－１９９７ (2nd Edition)
幸福鬼魂手记
杨炼新作１９９８－２００２
艳诗

YANG LIAN

杨炼

Riding Pisces

—Poems from Five Collections—

骑乘双鱼座：五诗集选

Translated by Brian Holton

The cover image (2006), dedicated to Yang Lian, is by Rebecca Horn.

Published in the United Kingdom in 2008 by
Shearsman Books Ltd
58 Velwell Road
Exeter EX4 4LD   www.shearsman.com

ISBN 978-1-905700-91-2

Translator's Acknowledgments
Brian Holton would like to thank Rosie Xie for her help in translating 'The Mask
That Can't be Taken Off' when time was running out, and Sean Golden for his
fine work on 'Someone Who Dies in a Vision'.

Acknowledgements
Except where specified otherwise, the English translations appear here for the
first time. The poems in Section 1 first appeared in *Non-Person Singular* (London:
Wellsweep Press, 1994), but some of the translations have been revised for this
edition; the Chinese texts in Section 2 first appeared in *Masks and Crocodile* (Sydney:
Wild Peony, 1990); the translations in Section 3 first appeared in *Painted Bride
Quarterly*, and were subsequently collected in *Notes of a Blissful Ghost* (Hong Kong:
Renditions, 2002); the majority of the translations in Section 4 first appeared in
Notes of a Blissful Ghost (Hong Kong: Renditions, 2002) and are reproduced here
by kind permission of Renditions and the Chinese University of Hong Kong; the
poems in Section 5 are published here for the first time except for 'Sailor's Home',
which first appeared (in both Chinese and English) in the anthology *Sailor's Home*,
edited by Yang Lian (Exeter: Shearsman Books, 2005).

CONTENTS

1. *from* NON-PERSON SINGULAR

5. *from* DARK BLUE POEMS

* Translated by W.N. Herbert and the author.

无人称

1. *from* Non-Person Singular

天葬

当石头梦见这些名字
我再一次死去
在那鼾声中步入静谧的房子
窗外有鸟　别处的叫声
和拖着鲜红尾线从地面驶过的早晨
我的脸会见另一张脸　一次碰撞
天空是花岗岩的
祖先走不出这小小洞穴
熄灭的炉火　只留下一把锤子
为了从黑暗中雕出海洋
日子的盲眼睁开
白骨深陷不移　虽然
石头梦见这些名字都是雪
静静融化
我梦见　那些鸟飞翔着渐渐是光
远离悬崖　梦见所有石头的梦

十一月版画

十一月有一具被烧焦的尸骸
在窗口摇晃
黑色的无力哭泣的光

十一月是被剥尽了外衣的核桃
黑色的无力哭泣的女人
酸雨中孤零零暴露的大脑

坠落　和你不分先后
整个早晨　黑色的田野
白的霜

白的马群　白花花的海流
与二月对称地逝去
在天上　黑暗中充满不哭的光

Sky Burial

as stones dream of these names
I die once again
stepping into that house of stillness) amid snoring
there are birds outside the window   cries of elsewhere
and the speeding-by morning dragging its mooring line over the ground
my face meets another face   a single collision
the sky is granite
our forefathers could not escape this tiny little cave
the dying flame   leaves behind just a hammer
for the ocean carved from darkness
day's blind eyes open
white bones sunken deep unmoving   even if
stones dream these names are all snow
tranquilly melting
I dream   of those birds wheeling imperceptibly into light
far from the cliffs   to dream the dreams of every stone

November Print

In November there's a charred corpse
swaying outside the window
a black weakly sobbing light

November is a walnut entirely stripped of its coating
a black weakly sobbing woman
a brain laid bare and alone in the acid rain

falling down   no earlier and no later than you
the whole morning   black fields
white frost

a white herd of horses   ocean currents flecked with white
passing away in symmetry with February
in the sky   darkness brimming with unsobbing light

雪

每当你觉得陌生就有雪来找你
那些诞生于一个肉体的光
把你淋湿　像这房间洁白无边的话语
在午夜你袒露如鸟
听着雪与雪第一次屈服于疯狂
隐入水　既然石头喝你
隐入刻你名字的手　在雪上在沙上
六种冰冷的天空片刻透明
你把自己投出去
像一再毁灭的日子该笑就笑
雪下着　你走后也下
或许是你在用熟悉的音乐找世界
隐入每个肉体上黑暗的墓穴
脱尽余毛　只有光
挥洒着纷飞的星群漫天如银
终极之白
神的赤裸是唯一的

房间里的风景

三十二岁　听够了谎言
再没有风景能够移进这个房间
长着玉米面孔的客人
站在门口叫卖腐烂的石头
展览舌苔　一种牙缝里磨碎的永恒

他们或你都很冷　冷得想
被呕吐　像墙上亵渎的图画
记忆是一小队渐弱的地址
秋之芒草　死于一只金黄的赤足
谁凭窗听见星群消失
这一夜风声　仿佛掉下来的梨子
空房间被扔出去

在你赤裸的肉体中徘徊又徘徊
肢解　如天空和水

SNOW

whenever you feel like a stranger, snow comes visiting you
these lights embodied in flesh
soak you through   like the endlessly, spotlessly white language of
                                            this room
at midnight you're stripped bare as a bird
as you listen to snow on snow, the first surrender to madness comes
hiding in water   since stones drink you
hiding in the hand that carves your name   on snow, on sand
six ice-cold heavens instantly transparent
you fling yourself out
laugh because you ought to, like the days that time and again are destroyed
snow is falling   falls, too, once you're gone
maybe it's you visiting the world with intimately-known music
hiding in the dark grave of all flesh
feathers quite cast off   there is only light
sprinkling whirling herds of stars like silver across the sky
ultimate white
nakedness of spirit is the only thing

THE LANDSCAPE IN THE ROOM

thirty-two years old   heard enough lying
no landscape can ever again enter this room
a corn-faced stranger
stands at the door hawking putrid stones
displaying tongue-fur   a kind of eternity ground between the teeth

they or you are both cold   cold enough to want
to be vomited up   like the profane pictures on the walls
memory is a whole squad of weakening addresses
autumn's bearded weeds   dead under a bare yellow-gold foot
Someone (leaning) by the window hears the herds of stars disappear
the night-long wind's sound   seems like falling pears
the empty room is thrown away

wavering and wavering again in your naked flesh
dismemberment   like sky and water

湿太阳　受伤吼叫时忘了一切
再没有风景能够入这片风景
弄死你

直到最后一只鸟也逃往天上
在那手中碰撞　冻结成蓝色静脉
你把自己锁在哪儿
这房间就固定在哪儿　空旷的回声
背诵黑暗
埋葬你心里唯一的风景唯一的

谎言

其时其地

那座我回不去的老房子
你也回不去了　虽然
那盏灯通宵亮着　听着窗外
白杨高大的黑影
你还在等　一阵荒凉的脚步声

整个秋天　只有风来拜访
一一翻动那些红瓦
十月的连翘花黯淡如败壁颓垣
却在一个晚上突入你的梦境
那时　谁将茕茕独自开放
在一座我回不去的熟悉的老房子
你回不去　陌生的旧日子

音乐的心悄悄停了
房子藏进它自己的忘却里
绿或睡眠包裹的树　一旦惊醒
已片片凋零

旧日子还在　我们的手消失之处
名字　移开　谨守同一禁忌
但每个清晨当鸟叫了
你是否记得有一个黑暗

wet sun   forgot everything as it howled in pain
no landscape can ever again enter this landscape
to do you to death

until the last bird has also escaped into the sky
colliding within that hand   frozen into blue veins
wherever you lock yourself
there the room is fixed   spacious echoes
recite the darkness
bury your heart's only landscape

lie

THE TIME, THE PLACE

that old house I can't go back to
you can't go back to now either   even though
as that lamp lights up the whole night   hearing outside the window
the poplars' tall black shadows
you're still waiting   for the desolate spatter of footsteps

the entire autumn   only the wind came visiting
upturning the red tiles one by one
October's forsythia faint as the crumbling of ruined walls
yet on one evening it came charging into your dream
then   who will bloom solitary and bright
in a familiar old house I can't go back to?
you can't go back   to those strange bygone days

the music's heart has quietly stopped
the room conceals itself in its own forgetting
trees wrapped in green or sleep   once awakened are
all withered, all fallen, all scattered

bygone days still exist   the place where our hands disappeared
names   move   carefully obeying identical taboos
but early each morning as the birds sang
did you remember there had been a darkness

自沉默中升起　倾倒出越来越远的
地平线　另外星球上深黄波荡的水纹
所有路溶解
这成了唯一的归途

纸鸟

房间就是这日子　冷漠的墙
耸起雪白波峰的暴风雨
而所有女病人们憔悴的脸色
都年代久远
横扫纸　鸟　飞翔在午后显得松脆

在看不见的河岸晾干躯体
沉入光　一个轻巧的黑黑的漩涡
张开翅膀
以死亡的形式诞生才真的诞生

一根手指支撑一个世界
纤细的骸骨精疲力竭
于是所停无处
房间或孩子的戏弄或空中
每个地址装饰着早被忘记的名字
主人走后　往事像绿锈斑驳的假牙
日子逃开你像梦逃开一片蓝

墙是最后的白影子
在流逝的皮肤深处　沙砾微微闪光
在耳朵们堆积的寂寞里
传来扑打声
漫长的黄昏足够渐渐贴近死亡

云　星　月　撕碎的羽毛
纷纷飞起
在没有你的时刻　找到你

rising from silence   overturning the ever farther
horizon?   on another planet the brown surge of rippling waters
all roads dissolve
this has become the only way home

PAPER BIRDS

the room is this day   indifferent walls
crest the storm towering over snow-white waves
and all the female patients' worn-out complexions
are distanced by the long passage of time
sweep over paper   birds   wheeling so crisply in the afternoon

on the invisible riverbank the wind-dried bodies
sink into light   a dexterous black whirlpool
spreads wings
the only true birth is born in death's shape

one finger supports a world
the slender skeleton is exhausted, spent
and so there is nowhere to rest
the room or the children's teasing or the air above
every address ornaments long-forgotten names
after the owner goes   the past is like green rust-stained false teeth
the day escapes you as dreams escape a patch of blue

the wall is the last white shadow
in the depths of elapsed skin   grit faintly gleams
in the silence heaped up by the ears
comes the sound of swatting
the long long twilight is ample enough to settle into death

cloud   star   moon   shredded feathers
fly up in crowds one after the other
in the instant you are not there   to find you

镜

倘若现实　能够从幻象开始
玻璃就是唯一的风景
门开着　水银的瀑布声
白昼弯曲后
与黑夜结盟的另一个白昼
从睫毛开始　月下
鹅卵石有淡黄的借据般的光泽

房间里的房间
拍卖无声进行
眼睛和半身像交换刻毒的愿望
蚂蚁爬过嘴角细碎的皱纹
野草横生
为皮肤和泥土深处那同一副枯骨
追逐　像准备冬眠的蛇
血是萧瑟的红叶林
每照亮一次就死亡一次

玻璃的沼泽　水银的稍纵即逝的飞鸟
俯身之际　脸僵硬成石
岁月布下迷宫让自己失传

我们在地下线下漂流
圆睁双眼
如鱼的四肢互相纠缠
穿过桥洞　世界高悬在头上
谁窥见自己
谁就得悲惨地诞生

水之居

黑暗在床外高悬　天空抬起你
炽热的白色
鸟叫了一声又深深沉默

Mirror

suppose reality   could begin from illusion
glass is the only landscape
as the door opens   the sound of a quicksilver waterfall
after daylight meanderings
another daylight in league with the dark
starting from the eyelashes   under the moon
cobblestones have the pale yellow gleam of IOU's

a room within a room
an auction goes silently on
the eye and the half-length portrait swap spiteful desires
broken laugh-lines climbed by ants
weeds proliferating
for the same dry bones in the depths of soil and skin
pursue   like a snake preparing for hibernation
blood is a forest of red leaves bleakly rustling
each illumination a dying

the swamp of glass   a quicksilver bird gone in an instant
as you lean into it   the face stiffens, turns to stone
years lost in the maze they spread

we drift below the horizon
open our eyes wide
entwined in four fishlike limbs
pass under the arch of a bridge   the world hangs high above us
whoever catches a glimpse of himself
has tragically to be brought to life

The House of Water

darkness hangs beyond the bed   the sky lifts you up
a blazing white
a bird cries once, then deep silence

如唇的海浪淋漓直下
暴露出隐匿的牙齿
咬疼沙滩　你的岛屿残缺不全
在风中漂流
让庞大的水族阵阵瘙痒游动
被逼近时猝然亮起　光或者盐

终于一个迫在眉睫
海水散开　深入你的是树
宛如喷泉的树
头晕目眩的白色波浪　横冲直撞
在你空荡荡的海底　溺死你

黑暗把你带走　你听不见
鸟儿做梦似的又开始叫了
枝头很远
而你还在这床上　孤零零地起伏
去世多年的母亲依然阵痛抽搐
没有什么　甚至没有你
一枝水仙持续的睡眠
阳光很远　那世界更远　更远

记忆中的女孩

深深地吸气　再闭上眼
你就来到我的房间
在夏日　荒草有歌曲的手指
和你的脚　一个静静墓园中的回忆

不　你别弯腰去看那墓碑
顽皮地找　和你一模一样的名字
别对她们低语　或者笑
那也曾被人记住的笑声

不不　那不是你
躺在上面晒太阳的青草地
一块九岁的织满了光的绿毯子
石头并不懂你热爱的一切

liplike the ocean waves drip down
to expose hidden teeth
painfully biting the beach   your islands incomplete fragments
drifting in the wind
making immense sea beasts itch to be on the move
when approached it suddenly lights up   light or salt

finally daybreak is urgent, imminent
the waters disperse   what enters deep in you is a tree
a tree like a fountain
dazzling, dizzying white breakers   wildly jolting and colliding
on your deserted seabed   drowning you

darkness bears you away   you can't hear
the birds' cries begin again, as if in a dream
the branches are far away
and you are still on this bed   rising and falling all alone
your mother, passed away these many years, twitches still in childbirth
there's nothing   there's not even you
the continuing sleep of the narcissus
the sunlight is far away   that world is farther still   farther still

A GIRL REMEMBERED

a deep breath   then eyes closed
and you come to my room
in summertime   there are fingers of song in the thickets
and your feet   a memory of a still cemetery

no   don't bend down to look at that headstone
mischievously seeking   a name identical to your own
don't whisper to them   or laugh
that laughter which others once remembered too

no   no   that's not
the grassy ground where you bathed in sunshine
a green carpet, a nine-year-old web filled with light
the stone doesn't understand the all you so deeply loved

名字四散各处　像小小的风
来自你　又在你的呼吸之外做着梦
在不远的地下被忘却
或很远　走进这想你而你从未来过的房间

戈雅一生的最后房间

最后　这房间远去　一只狗
逃到沙下喝汤　喝　骷髅的汤匙里
唯一的液体

终于漂浮成一幅无人风景
阴暗的沼泽上　灌木丛抹杀天空
飞鸟在痛苦
哀号已无力搅扰大地

魔女们聚集如一片柔软的花朵
向山羊盛开鲜艳的器官
在庆典中舞蹈　只有死鱼曾经活过
眼珠白花花瞪着
崩溃

没人懂得　这黑色石榴的硕大头颅
浮肿并烂掉了耳朵
那被听见的寂静怎样夷平一生
岁月怎样　成了更换丧服的房子

而肉里是一块木头干燥　劈裂的声音
把聋子钉在墙上
四肢爬动　结着网
死者鱼贯而入　张大受惊的鼻孔

末日接踵而至　一节风干的骨髓
形似手的弦
于阵阵嘶鸣之后　松弛　哑默

现在　是这墙长满了耳朵
却已不听　烛光幽幽远远扩散的风暴

names scattered all around   like the faintest breeze
coming from you   and dreaming beyond your breath
forgotten below the undistant ground
or far distant   entering this room that thinks of you, to which you
                                            have never come

The Last Room in Goya's Life

finally   the room goes far away   a dog
escapes to drink soup under the sand   drinks   from a skull spoon
the one and only liquid

floating at last into an unpeopled landscape
in the gloomy swamp   bushes and thickets blot out the sky
flying birds in pain
wail piteously with no power to disturb the earth

devil women gather like a lithe and flexible flower
their organs blooming brightly at the goats
dancing in celebration   only the dead fish was ever alive
eyeballs staring, glistening white
they collapse

no one understands   this gigantic black pomegranate head
dropsical, with ears rotted away
how that heard silence razes a life
how the years   become a house for putting on mourning
and how timber dries in the flesh   sounds of splitting
nail the deaf man to the wall
limbs scramble   weave a net
the dead file in   flaring frightened nostrils

the last days arrive one after another   a length of wind-dried bone
                                            marrow
formed like the strings of a hand
after the waves of hoarse cries   flaccidity   dumb silence

now   this wall is grown full of ears
that no longer listen   to the storm, diffused to distance and dimness
                                            by candlelight

23

这笔触遍布盲点
像一张张无声咧开的嘴
吞咽着孤独的石头
在深处　形同渊薮　便挥霍整个世界
直到房间里挤满素不相识的鬼魂
绕床而歌　不朽于某个人垂死的一刻
——世界　当你不能理解时
你聆听吧

this pen spreads blind spots
like mouths wide open in a silent grin
swallowing the stone of solitude
in depths   lair-shaped   the entire world is squandered
until the room is packed with wholly unacquainted ghosts
singing around the bed   immortal in someone's dying instant
—world   when you cannot understand
just listen!

一九八九年

谁说死者会互相拥抱
像一匹匹马　鬃毛银灰
站在窗外结冰的月光中
死者埋进过去的日子
刚刚过去　疯子就被绑在床上
僵直如铁钉
钉着黑暗的木头
棺盖每天就这样合拢

谁说死者已死去　死者
关在末日里流浪是永久的主人
四堵墙上有四张自己的脸
再屠杀一次　血
仍是唯一著名的风景
睡进坟墓有福了　却又醒在
一个鸟儿更怕的明天
这无非是普普通通的一年

1989

who says the dead can embrace?
like fine horses   manes silver grey
standing outside the window in the freezing moonlight
the dead are buried in the days of the past
in days not long past   madmen were tied onto beds
rigid as iron nails
pinning down the timbers of darkness
the coffin lid each day closing over like this

who says the dead are dead and gone?   the dead
enclosed in the vagrancy of their final days
are the masters of forever
four faces of their own on four walls
butchery yet again   blood
is still the only famous landscape
slept into the tomb they were lucky   but they wake again in
a tomorrow the birds fear even more
this is no doubt a perfectly ordinary year

谎言背后 （四首）

给一个大屠杀中猝死的九岁女孩

他们说一根红皮筋把你绊倒了
你跳出白粉笔的房子
雨声响得怕人的日子

九个弹坑在你身上发甜
他们说你把月亮玩丢了
墓草青青　是新换的牙齿

在一个无须哀悼的地方萌芽
你没死　他们说
你还坐在小木桌后边

目光碰响黑板
下课铃骤然射击
一阵空白　你的死被杀死

他们说　现在　你是女人是母亲
每年有个没有你的生日
像生前那样

死角

你扑倒的地方一片空白
而黑暗中的躯体
弯成死角

枪声躲在里面哭泣
名字躲进更里边　胆怯得
希望被忘记

没入每个人
每个夜晚
在零点　重新滴血

BEHIND THE LIES

1. FOR A NINE-YEAR-OLD GIRL KILLED IN THE MASSACRE

they say you were tripped by a strip of red elastic
as you skipped from the square of white chalk
on a day of frighteningly loud rain

on your body nine bullet holes grew sweet
they say you played with the moon until you lost it
grass green on the grave   the new teeth you grew

budding in a place where grief is not needed
you didn't die   they say
you still sit behind a little wooden desk

vision clatters against the blackboard
the recess bell, astonishingly, is loosed off
a blast of blank space   your death is killed

they say   now   you are a woman, a mother
each year there is a birthday without you
the way it was when you were alive

2. DEATH'S ANGLE

a blank, the place where you fell forward
and the body in the dark
bent into death's angle

gunshots hide inside, weeping
names hide still further in   so timid they
hope to be forgotten

submerging everyone
each evening
at zero hour   dripping blood again

天堂的血迹

此刻天使的笑声是枪声
笑出眼泪　血色的黎明
地下室里一场冷雨

魔鬼们环绕一棵菊花烤火
咒骂六月的坏天气
下水道疯了　残肢涌出
落月和冰雹的腥臭淤泥
汤匙捞起一只聋耳
反正死亡是不透明的

天使坐在铁椅子上笑
天使的笑声击落飞鸟
楼上楼下

死者裸体如一条条舌头
被黑猫在墙角追逐
被忘却的时辰再屠杀一次
菊花看见
每个地址上一座骨头花园
反正死亡是不透明的

血流去　在黎明消失
死亡哈哈大笑
天堂明亮地舔着嘴唇

腐烂的笑声里菊花开着
枪声在紧闭的门背后
敲响无血的躯体
这聋子世界唯一一摊血迹
天使和魔鬼在碰杯
反正死亡是不透明的

3. BLOODSTAINS IN HEAVEN

in this moment the laughing of angels is gunfire
laughing tears   a bloody daybreak
cold rainfall in the cellars

devils warm themselves around a chrysanthemum
cursing the bad June weather
gutters are going crazy   spewing out severed limbs
the stinking ooze of hailstones and the setting moon
the soupspoons lift out a deaf ear
death is not transparent, anyway

angels sit in iron chairs, laughing
the laughter of angels shoots the flying birds down
above stairs and below

the dead, naked as tongues
are chased by black cats into a corner
massacred once again by the instant of forgetting
chrysanthemums see
a bone-garden at every address
death is not transparent, anyway

blood flows away   vanishes at daybreak
the dead roar with laughter
heaven shiningly licks its lips

chrysanthemums open amid the sound of decomposing laughter
gunfire behind a door tightly shut
knocks on bloodless bodies
this deaf world the sole beach of bloodstains
angels and devils clink their glasses
death is not transparent, anyway

失踪

冗长的一生仅有两个时辰
死亡　然后被遗忘
终于我在众多面孔中成了真空

那个夜晚比死亡更深邃
枪杀没有声音　火越烧越冷
所有躯体被轻轻敲碎
而所有的血揭示一种白
像不再归来的名字
石头隧道大口咽下鲜红的泥泞

那个夜晚就此失传
影子挥舞而手臂脱落
天空眩目　可眼睛融解
言辞秘密走动　嘴
埋入地下　阳光繁衍成公开的禁忌

我死在第二次　在早晨
密布枪眼的脸再次密布字眼
更黑的弹洞是这个白昼
更放肆的屠杀　谎言剥光死者
直到我只能不真实地活着

那不被承认的末日只能无所不在

同时所有人真实地死去
我的血肉失踪成陌生人的血肉
被删改的死亡删改着生命
众多面孔因此真空因此白骨嶙峋
每颗头颅成为一座坟墓
最深的埋葬拥有一切死亡
像遗忘　用鲜红的泥泞洗手
用饱和的沉默过滤
当尸体最后被偷走　那夜晚永存

在时间之外
我回来　继续死去

4. Missing

there are only two hours in this long and tedious life
dying   and then being forgotten
in the end I am a vacuum in the multitude of faces

that night was more obscure than death
the fatal shots were silent   fire burned ever colder
all the bodies were gently tapped to pieces
and all the blood announced a kind of white
like a name that never came home
the great maw of the stone tunnel swallowed the scarlet mud

that night is lost to history now
shadows waved, but their arms fell off
the sky was dizzy   yet eyes melted
the spoken word walked secretly about   mouths
buried underground   sunlight multiplied into overt taboo

I died for the second time   in the morning
my face pocked with bullet holes, pocked over again with phraseology
bright day an even blacker entrance wound
a still more wanton slaughter   lies stripped the dead bare
till I could only live a bogus, inauthentic life

that unacknowledged dying day has to be ever-present, everywhere

at the same time as everyone died an authentic death
my flesh and blood went missing, became someone else's flesh and blood
revised death revising life
so the multitude of faces were a vacuum, white bone jagged and thin
each skull becoming a tomb
the deepest burials possessing all death
like forgetting   washing the hands with scarlet mud
filtered through saturated silence
as the corpses were finally stolen   that night was eternal

outside of time
I come back   to carry on dying

流亡之书

你不在这里　这笔迹
刚刚写下就被一阵狂风卷走
空白如死鸟在你脸上飞翔
送葬的月亮一只断手
把你的日子向回翻动
翻到你缺席的那一页
你一边书写一边
欣赏自己被删去

像别人的声音
碎骨头随随便便碎到角落里
水和水摩擦的空洞声音
随随便便移入呼吸
移入一只梨就不看别人
一地头颅都是你
在字里行间一夜衰老
你的诗隐身穿过世界

被禁止的诗

死在三十五岁已经太迟
你早该在子宫中被处决
像你的诗　无须
一页白纸作墓地

不准诞生的孩子
把手锁在罪恶里
五指腐烂像冬眠中纠缠的蛇
眼睛腐烂　逃开噬人的风暴
你的脸一摸就是一汪水
骨头划出道道白痕

是肉体深海下一群鳗鱼
在白色海草间穿游
更苍白的呼喊间只听见黑暗
你被别的手无情抹平
淡淡改成一个错字

THE BOOK OF EXILE

you are not here   this pen mark
just written is blown away by the gale
is blank as if a dead bird circled above your face
the funeral-following moon a broken hand
turns your days backward
turns to the page where you are absent
as you write   so you are
a connoisseur of your own excision

like the sound of someone else
crushed bones casually spat into a corner
the hollow sound of water clashing on water
casually moving into a breath
into a pear so no-one else need be seen
the skulls on the ground are all you
growing old overnight between the words, the lines
your poem has invisibly pierced the world

BANNED POEM

to die at thirty-five is already too late
you should have been executed in the womb
like your poem   no need
for a grave made from one sheet of white paper

children not permitted to be born
lock up their hands in crime
fingers rot like snakes coiled in winter sleep
eyes rot   escaping the tempest that bites
your face at first touch is a current of water
bones tracing out white scars line by line

it's a shoal of eels down in the deep waters of the flesh
threading through white seaweed
among still-paler shouts you hear only darkness
coldly wiped clean by another hand
coolly turned into a misprint

胎衣越裹越紧
遗言和你一同死去

死在今天
变成一个恶臭的消息

众目

我们在众目睽睽下赤裸
被流放于黑暗躯体
这一夜　诞生了所有星光

海潮把沙滩卷走
我们在众目睽睽下飞起
比羽毛还轻

倒挂上天空
被星际灼热的累累碎石
冻伤双脚

黑暗中空白的脚印
雨滴心脏都漫步着化为石头
我们被撕开　于是远远死去

孩子化为水依旧干渴
梦化为刺客的手
尸骸交叉搭成拱顶

这么多星狂暴地毁灭这么多神
这么多光年片刻融化
如雪花

一刹那忘却
黑夜从未溢出眼眶
世界新得如此残忍

听任光舔净
黑暗浪头上的鸟群
我们在众目睽睽下失传

placenta wrapping you ever tighter
your last words dying with you

to die today
turning into a stinking news story

THE PUBLIC EYE

we are naked in the public eye's gaze
exiled in these dark bodies
on this night   all starlight is born

seatides roll the beach away
we are flying up in the public eye's gaze
lighter than feathers

hanging upside down in the sky
feet frost-bitten
by the countless shattered stones blazing in the firmament

a blank footprint in the dark
raindrop hearts both turn to stone as we stroll
we are ripped apart   then die so far away

children turn to water and are still thirsty
dreams turn to assassin's hands
entwined skeletons build up a vault above

so many stars violently wiping out so many gods
so many light-years melting in an instant
like snowflakes

forget in a flash
night has still not overflowed the eye-sockets
the world is this ruthless because it's so new

let the light lick clean
the flocks of birds on the waves of darkness
we are lost in the public eye's gaze

老人
——三十五岁自赠

年轻时我们做梦　说谎
如今老了才听见
寂静在裂开
才懂得　我们都是盲人
一生的病
是抚摸一个变幻不定的字
才看清陈年的家具
是等待收尸的护士
关切地站在周围
也老了
血管里那口钟硬了
绿漆剥落的月亮在墙上
海萎缩成木纹
海鸥点点灰白的指甲
掐进岁月
掐算着别人的笑声
只有衰老
才使我们从野狗猩红的目光中
数清自己骸骨上
残存多少干枯的
肉

虚空中的雕塑

其实没有路
通向我曾呼吸的地方

当一张早晨的床
被许多年的往事淹没
风冻结在空中
星群在灰蓝的纸背面闪烁
翻过去　世界
就再次被洗劫干净

OLD MAN

(for myself, on my 35th birthday)

in youth we dream   tell lies
only now, grown old, do we hear
silence splitting open
only now understand   we're all blind
a lifelong disease
is touching an unstable, varying word
only then do we see the worn furniture clearly
it's the nurses who wait to lay out the corpse
standing attentively around us
and grown old too
that bell in the veins has hardened
a peeling green-painted moon on the wall
the sea has shrivelled into woodgrain
the pallid nails of the seagulls
grip deep into the years
with the sound of laughter that tells another's fortune
only decrepitude
lets us count up on our own skeleton
with the bloodshot eyes of a wild dog
how much withered flesh
remains

SCULPTURE IN THE VOID

in fact there are no roads
leading to the place where I once breathed

on a morning bed
submerged in years of the past
the wind freezes in the sky
herds of stars gleam on the back of grey-blue paper
turned over   the world
is looted and emptied once again

死于记忆
每天重犯的无辜罪行
无知的头颅
坠入　一场渺无人迹的战争

绿色的田野　一个更沉重的惩罚
等待　身体的枯井中
不可能涌出的泉水
覆盖在明亮残忍的鸟声下
分手时不属于任何人的时刻
乌有的时刻
隔开一分钟　已隔开永恒

凿穿黑暗与空白边缘的手
也把我雕成另一个人
僵尸幽暗的齿缝里
名字每天上演
一场越来越远的大屠杀
远在内心里
篡改一滴血
床　比人类更熟悉
切开动脉后混浊的
呻吟

谁也不是胜利者
我们或时间
回不去昨天　自己却成为昨天
封存在石头里的视线
纠缠成唯一的墓地

死于记忆
与死于忘却一样
死者仅拥有
任石头回忆的
自由

death in memory
an innocent offence repeated daily
the ignorant skull
dropping into   a distant uninhabited war

green fields   a heavier punishment
awaits in the dry wells of the body
spring water that can't gush forth
is capped under cruel shining birdsong
at parting, the moment which belongs to nobody
a non-existent moment
partitions a minute   has partitioned eternity

the hand that drilled through darkness and the blank border
has carved me into someone else too
in the gloomy cracks between the corpses' teeth
names perform every day
a more and more distant massacre
far off in the heart
distort a drop of blood
beds   more familiar than humans
with the indistinct groans
after the artery is cut open

no-one is the victor
neither us or time
no-one can go back to yesterday   though we have become yesterday
a line of sight sealed in stone
tangles in the only grave

death in memory
is the same as death in forgetfulness
yet the dead possess
a freedom which allows for the memories
of stones

老故事（五首）

老故事 （一）

每天早上收拾房间
像精心布置死后的风景
打开收音机 战争
就在咫尺之内进行

灰尘从一张女人肖像上脱落
那款式新颖的假牙
暴露出零星星的骨骼
整整一个世纪微笑着手淫

阳光也老了　笔直地撞墙
面对这世界视而不见
条纹睡衣搭上床头
里面有鸟声　酒迹斑斑

有人开始问候
有人开始剪草坪
九点整　早餐端上来了
今天谁将出卖我们

老故事 　（三）

那孩子生在马槽里
冷月下空荡荡的海底
被三个垂死的老头子
恶狠狠诅咒

四季不过是一道转门
尸首沉溺　喂肥五彩珊瑚间的鱼
出入超级市场　你模仿
土豆　圣贤似的严厉咳嗽

熟读讨价还价的惊险情节
用一根牙签剔净自己

OLD STORIES

OLD STORY 1

every morning I tidy the room
as if meticulously re-arranging the landscape after a death
switch on the radio   war
goes on within arm's length

dust falls from the portrait of a woman
these new-style false teeth
disclose skeletons scattered here and there
an entire century smiling as it masturbates

the sunlight has aged too   striking the wall dead straight
unnoticed as it faces this world
striped pyjamas hang on the bed-head
birdsong inside   spotted with wine-stains

people start to greet each other
people start to mow the lawn
nine o'clock precisely   breakfast is served
who will betray and sell us out today?

OLD STORY 2

that child was born in a manger
a deserted ocean floor under a cold moon
by three moribund old codgers
given a ferocious benediction

the seasons, though, are a revolving door
corpses drown   feed fat fish among coloured coral
in and out of the supermarket   you imitate
a potato   cough strictly like a saint

a skilled reader of the thrill of haggling
with a toothpick you pick yourself clean

你在橱窗里触礁了多次
已拥有足够的智慧

把别人带出沙漠
让神　安葬于天空
海底有钟表　却没有时间
有你　却没有人

老故事　（三）

三十岁是一扇开向疯狂的门
另一条街等待我
路灯和黄昏　从四面八方拷打
影子影子一小片沙漠

三十岁　像盘子油腻无光
窗口照例审问
下班后精疲力竭的骸骨
食肉的玻璃保持着饥饿

脸　嚼
平坦的头发下　那平坦的空白
死亡流行色统一后
填进表格的一生

另一条街上没人行走
也没手指　触摸麻风病中的绿草地
回家的时候　只想到
床　最后一个奇迹

老故事（四）

楼梯的诡秘尸体倒在黑暗中
地毯上一百年的足迹
不孤独　彼此磨破了皮肤
听着窗外同一场暴风雨

you've struck many a reef in the display cases
therefore now you possess enough wisdom

to lead someone else out of the desert
let god   be buried in the sky
there are timepieces on the ocean floor   but no time
there is you   but there is no person

Old Story 3

thirty is a door opening on madness
yet another street awaits me
streetlamps and twilight   from all sides thrash
the shadows, the shadows a small stretch of desert

thirty   like dull grease on a plate
the window, as usual, interrogates
the skeleton knackered after a day's work
the carnivorous glass   holds on to its hunger

the face   chews
below the cropped hair   that cropped blank
once unified by the popular colour of death
a whole life is filled in on forms

on yet another street no-one is walking
no fingers, either   touch the green leprous lawn
when you go back home   think only of
bed   the final miracle

Old Story 4

the stair's secret corpse falls in the darkness
on the carpet a hundred years of footprints
not alone   between them they've worn skin away
as they listened to the rainstorm outside the window

肉里一滴滴漏满了夜
夏天的年轮间散发出霉味
鸟卡在锁孔中
而梦　推开一道虚掩的门

死者都活着
昏暗的角落　昨天用不同口音
谈论末日那冗长的话题
一面镜子盛满月光像一座老房子

却已忘了谁来过　谁走了
所有影子停在身体里
窗外的暴风雨渐渐逼入窗内
百年逼入这一瞬　我正死去

老故事（五）

当你醒时天空僵硬
一生写下的字迹群星散去
骨节里阵阵风声
你被翻动　如一页疯狂的白纸

记忆中的名字都不看你
两扇相邻的窗户
推开你脸上两个无关的春天
老太阳说　凡距离皆无垠

你的呼吸之外　遍布胆小的死者
逃犯一再更换地址
树木不可触摸的绿更换日子
凡致命的蓝皆漆黑

老太阳坠入蛆虫潮湿的眼神
谁都不在这里　你钉在
没人讲述的故事上
每天复活　玷污着白昼

drip by drip, night has leaked in to fill the flesh
from between the growth rings of the summer rises the smell of
mildew
birds are wedged into the holes of the locks
and dreams   push open an unlatched door

the dead are all alive
the dim corner   yesterday in a different voice
discussed the long and tedious topic of our dying day
a mirror flooded with moonlight is like an old house

but we've forgotten that whoever came   and went
all shadows stop in the body
the rainstorm outside the window forces its way inside
a century forces its way into this instant   I am dying, here and now

Old Story 5

as you wake   the sky is rigid
stars scatter a lifetime's handwriting
in your joints the sound of blustery wind
you're turned over   like an insane sheet of white paper

all names in your memory stop looking at you
two neighbouring windows
push two irrelevant springtimes open in your face
old sun says   every distance is limitless

beyond your breathing   the timid dead are everywhere
escaped convicts time and again change addresses
the untouchable green of the trees changes days
every fatal blue is pitch black

old sun sinks into the moist look of maggots
there's no-one here   you are nailed to
a story no-one tells
resurrected each morning   to sully the daylight

冬日花园

1

树木在雪中冻红　像穿着破旧的风衣
雪在脚下吱嘎作响
匆匆行走的夜总有一双簇新的鞋底

山羊们害怕孤寂　就为每只耳朵
把叫声变成一片痛哭

道路　一条刚刚产仔的母牛
浑身鞭痕地瘫痪在泥血中喘息

路灯亮得更早了　情人幽暗如石头
站在金属灵床边面目模糊
田鼠是一位疲倦的护士　偷偷
缩进花园的伤口做梦
花朵　在地下保存着淡红色的肉
像孩子死去后　一直鲜嫩的鬼魂

发育不全的星星　用铁栏杆锁住我们

2

世界上最不信任文字的　是诗人
空白的雪中　玫瑰从诞生就枯萎了
火焰远离一双寒冷的手
冬天忙碌着　像个勤奋的编辑
我　成为被阳光剪掉的
俯身嗅着自己日渐浓郁的尸臭
一个人的北风中　花园久已逝去

为幻象而存在　最后仍旧归于幻象
树和树的蓝色音乐　只由寂静来演奏
于是同一场大雪两次从我肩头落下
覆盖花园时　我是被忘记的
践踏一个路口　我是被弄错的
灯下空无一人的街像条沙哑的喉咙
朗诵着　而凋谢的辞旁观多年

THE GARDEN ON A WINTER'S DAY

1

trees frozen red in the snow   as if wearing worn-out windcheaters
snow crunching underfoot
the hurried night always wears brand-new soles

goats fear loneliness   for every ear
cries become bitter weeping

the path   a cow, just dropped a calf
scarred head to tail by the whip, panting paralysed in bloody mud

streetlamps come on still earlier   lovers dim as stones
stand, faces blurred, by a metal bier
the vole is an exhausted nurse   stealthily
slinking into the garden's wounds to dream
flowers   are preserving their pink flesh below ground
like dead children   straightaway, fresh tender ghosts

underdeveloped stars   lock us up with iron railings

2

in this world the ones who trust writing least   are poets
in the blank snow   roses have been withering since birth
the flame is far away from two cold hands
winter bustles about   like an industrious editor
I   become something spiked by the sunlight
bending to sniff at my death-stench which grows daily stronger
in one man's north wind   the garden long ago ceased to be

existing for illusion   in the end, as always, returning to illusion
the blue music of tree and tree   is played only by silence
so the same heavy snow has twice fallen on my shoulders
when it covers the garden   I am forgotten
stepping on an intersection   I am mistaken
under the lamps the empty street is like a hoarse throat
declaiming   and for years the withered and fallen words look on

3
有恋尸癖的人　爱在冬天漫步花园
向废墟行礼的人　能够欣赏
一个把小猫淹死在水沟里的阴谋
按下它的头像按碎一枚胡桃的
准是孩子　跑进花园的孩子

孩子比任何人更懂得如何踩躏花朵

连末日的也是假的　一截烧焦的木桩
像鳄鱼的长嘴斜斜探出地面
天空灰暗得像白昼的睡眠
大海吐出的鱼骨　也把我们刺疼
梦中一条条刮掉鳞片的鲜鱼活着刺疼
活在一把刀的行走下

每具肉体沦为一个无力回顾的地点

摸　这摸到的都是不在的
而毒瘤在深处摸不到地肿大
一个黑色的孕妇　包裹着被强奸的春天
一片目光劈开树干
天鹅的脖子弯成水底惨白的圈套
我们用分裂复眼的方式肢解世界后
都成了盲人　彼此的幽灵反衬出白雪
暴露于结冰的风中
忍受骨头抽芽的痛苦

直到　花园耻辱得不得不鲜艳
被一个不可辨认的季节抽打终生

3

some people, addicted to corpses   love to stroll in winter gardens
people who salute ruins   can appreciate
a plot to drown a kitten in a ditch
they who press its head down like crushing a walnut
are definitely children   children running into the garden

children know better than anyone how to trample flowers

even our dying day is unreal   a piece of a charred pole
poking slantwise from the ground like the crocodile's long snout
the sky is so gloomy it seems like daylight sleep
fishbones vomited by the ocean   stab us too
in dreams live fish, scraped clean of scales, are stabbed one by one
alive beneath the travelling knife

all flesh is reduced to a place with no power to look back

touch   all that is touched is non-existent
and cancer swells impalpably in the depths
a black pregnant woman   enwrapping a raped springtime
a treetrunk sliced by sight
swans' necks become pale underwater snares
once we have divided the world with fractured compound eyes
we are all blind   each spectre sets the white snow off
exposed in the dry ice-hard wind
endures the pain of bones budding

until   the garden is shamed into colour
lashed all its life by an unidentifiable season

格拉夫顿桥

桥下的墓地　　在你过桥时　　逼近
松树抬起一张张狐疑的脸
死者的海面　　铁块般散发腥味
铁锈色的阳光绕过去
像一只老狗嗅嗅你
一只狗眼盯着　　风景在桥上格外清晰

死火山萎缩的天空　　一个暗红的拳头
廉价墓碑上一滴过时的血
云　　汇合了昨天所有的风暴
却被鸟爪弄脏

被带你回家的栏杆　　敞开透明的窗户
你在家里过桥
整整一座城市住进一间病房
碧绿的野草把那么多脚步连在一起
石头的主人在石头屋顶下逼近
铁的主人在铁的走廊里逼近
用眼睛幻想　　死亡就无须速度
你走去的还是你被变老的那一端
草地上的死者俯瞰你　　是相同的距离

而你得回来　　像被玻璃手铐铐着
检修每座今天的罪恶的桥墩
一群雪白的海鸥里一个狂奔的孩子
突然站住　　为星星高呼
为黑夜中陡然延长的疼痛　　放声哭泣

战争纪念馆

永远　　火焰是火焰　　玫瑰是玫瑰
死亡　　仅仅让你们的肉体难堪
石头脸颊上的雕花玻璃　　像一个眼球
慢慢突起　　炸裂
一刹那崩溃后
谁也无力弥留崩溃的疼痛

GRAFTON BRIDGE

as you cross   the cemetery beneath the bridge   closes in
pinetrees raise suspicious faces
an ocean of the dead   giving off a fishy smell like iron
the rusty sunlight has passed by
sniffs at you like an old dog
a dog staring   the scene is particularly clear from the bridge

a sky shrivelled by extinct volcanoes   a dark red fist
a drop of the past's blood on a low-budget headstone
clouds   merge into yesterday's storm
and are fouled by the claws of birds

transparent windows opened   by the balustrade that brought you home
you cross the bridge at home
an entire city lodged in a sickroom
green weeds linking so many feet together
under a stone roof the stone master closes in
in an iron corridor the iron master closes in
fantasizing with the eyes   so death need not speed
the end you go to is always where you grow old
the dead on the lawn looking down at you   are all the same distance away

but you have to come back   as though fettered by handcuffs of glass
to overhaul every pier of today's sins
a child running crazy among snow-white seagulls
standing suddenly still   crying loudly for the stars
with a pain abruptly extended in the night   bitterly weeping

WAR MEMORIAL

always   the flame is a flame   the rose a rose
death   merely makes your bodies ill at ease
rose window on the stone face   like an eyeball
slowly protrudes   explodes
after that instantaneous collapse
no-one has the power to prolong the pain of collapsing

这座拦腰折断的塔是向下的
当月光　每个午夜被唱片变得刺耳
钟声　不耐烦地挥手把醉汉赶走
血　也能像草一样麻木
让聋子们席地而坐　浸透贱卖的香水

断壁残垣　在一片烛光外狂奔

石雕头朝下摔碎时　景色也颠倒了
婴儿从爆破的腹部　春天一样大声啼哭
管风琴继承了冒烟的喉咙
天空　却从来没有母亲

这张脸上的肉　总是刚刚扭歪的
鸽子不像雪白的弹片
像一枚枚骰子　朝镀金的轮盘掷去
黑夜是你们每天倒空的口袋

每认输一次你们就走下另一级台阶

被锁进另一间水泥浇铸的地下室
展览一件使自己失传的艺术
那儿　孩子用天真的瞳孔继续射击
一个城市的毁灭交给另一双小手
只是一件玩具　让你们重新玩
在时而火焰时而玫瑰的肉体深处玩
火焰和玫瑰互相遗忘
这座塔太高了　你们只能孤单地死去

钟声

敲了这么久　钟声早该是一根朽木
一颗俯瞰众人左右摇晃的脑袋

捂紧的耳朵　在手中腐烂
天空的圆形剧场　被这盏脚灯照亮

that broken-backed tower is upside down
as moonlight   each midnight turns shrill with records
the sound of bells   impatiently waves the drunkards away
blood   can also be as numb as the grass
let the deaf sit on the ground   slowly soak in cheap perfume

fragments of broken walls   run wild beyond the candlelight

when carved stone heads are dashed down   the landscape is also inverted
from an exploded belly a baby   wails like the spring
pipe organs inherit smoking throats
the sky, though   never had a mother

the flesh on this face   is always newly twisted
the doves are not like snow-white shrapnel
but like dice   cast on a gilded wheel
night is the pocket you turn out every day

each time you admit defeat you go down another flight of steps

locked into another concrete cellar
exhibiting art which will lose you yourself
there   a child goes on shooting with innocent eyes
the devastation of a city given over to other little hands
it's only a toy   you play with all over again
play in the depths of flesh that is now flame, now rose
flame and rose forget each other
this tower is too tall   all you can do is die alone

THE SOUND OF BELLS

struck so long   the sound of bells ought to have been rotten wood
                                                          long ago
a brain looking down on everyone tottering to and from

tightly stopped ears   rotting in the hand
the circular arena of the sky   lit up by these footlights

55

用一个罪名凭空捏造出世界
每天同样的脸色

乌鸦盘旋时　融化在打成死结的水里
钟声响起　每一下把你挪远一点

你不敢动也被挪远　像春天
孩子飞跑着穿过泥水　不在乎鞋袜

墓碑　佩带着常青藤族徽
躯体　被饥饿的服装一再更换

钟声是一个地点　让你和死者交谈
坐在岩石里猜想

那刚刚敲过的　是被阳光割掉的舌头
还没响起的　是鬼魂们住腻的房子

此刻　寂静急促　像最后一次呼吸
这个神垂死　他在向哪些神无辞地祈祷

谎言游戏

我们说谎时　老虎的条纹划动黑夜
道路　自从被灯光无情出卖
谎言　就代替行人

我们散步　而一只闯进梦呓禁区的蚂蚁
却不得不懂　手指
月亮每次落下时致命的重量
和　某条细小喉咙里愚蠢的呼救声

不　没人曾对自己说谎
只有辞句跟自己玩
玩着睡眠　我们就梦见大海
玩着大海　我们就漂向另一个岛屿
在那里登陆　我们饿了

to trump up a world with an accusation
each day's face the same expression

as crows circle   melt into tightly-knotted water
the bells sound   each stroke shifting you a little further

you daren't move but are shifted   like the springtime
children run flying through the mud   never heeding their socks

tombstones   wearing ancestral insignia of long green vines
bodies   changed time and again by hungry clothes

the sound of bells is a place   let you and the dead converse
sitting inside the rock speculating

what just struck there   is a tongue cut out by the sunlight
what still hasn't rung   is a house ghosts are sick of living in

in this instant   rapid silence   like the very last breath
this god is on his deathbed   to which gods is he wordlessly praying?

The Lying Game

when we lie   tiger stripes mark the night
since the roads   were shamelessly sold by the lamplight
lies   then replace travellers

we go strolling   yet an ant rushing into the forbidden zone of sleep-talk
has to understand   fingers
the mortal weight of the moon at each setting
and   idiotic cries for help in a certain tiny throat

no   no-one has ever lied to himself
it was just the words playing with themselves
playing at sleep   we dream of oceans
playing at oceans   we drift toward another islet
disembark there   we are hungry

就饲养或屠杀鹦鹉和猴子
重新变成凶猛的石头

可我们不说　我们不说时
两只手变成死水中互相咬住尾巴的鳄鱼

我们以为欺骗自己的那些话　只是
真的　每一行诗里的末日
是保存一张脸的摔碎多年的镜子
低低的耳垂
挂在男孩子滚动的铁环上

一生的太阳都向一个黑夜的陡坡滚去

当辞滚下来时　哑巴诞生了
哑巴心里疯狂的沉默
是一头老虎扑向羚羊时内心的沉默
肉被撕裂　甚至发不出纸的声音
我们从来都是哑巴
因此　被谎言当作玩具

死诗人的城

并非只有活过的人　才配去死
那些医生埋在寂静下的名字
签署了寂静　这座被你亲手瓜分的城
一条空旷的街伪装成送葬的队伍
而月光铁一般坚硬
白铁皮的手心里骨头哐哐响
早被忘记的窗外　小鼓咚咚响
你生前删掉的每个字回来删掉你

毫不吝惜地删　狠狠地删
删去世界后　标本中的脸更近更清晰
删去眼睛　目光就擦亮沿途的玻璃
雕刻一只线条纤细的鸟
像你看着它被打碎的那一只
被揉皱　丢弃　墙角腐烂的手稿上
你最后的死已经很熟悉
一间等待移出死亡残骸的老屋子

rear or butcher monkey and parrot
are turned afresh into savage stones

but we don't speak   when we don't speak
our hands become crocodiles biting each other's tails in dead water

we think the speech which deceives us   is only
truth   the dying day in every line of poetry
is a mirror, smashed years ago, preserving a face
drooping earlobes
hang on a boy's trundling hoop

a lifetime's suns are trundling down night's steep slope

when words come trundling down   mutes are born
the mad silence in the heart of a mute
is the silence in the tiger's heart as it springs on the gazelle
flesh is ripped   can't even make the noise of paper
we have always been mutes
and so   we are playthings for lies

CITY OF DEAD POETS

by no means only those who have lived   deserve to die
those names buried lifelong beneath silence
have signed the silence   this city you split with your own hand
a deserted street pretending to be a funeral procession
and moonlight hard as iron
bones clang in galvanised palms
outside long-forgotten windows   snare drums rattle
every word you deleted in your life comes back to delete you

unstintingly deletes   wolfishly deletes
the world deleted   the face among the specimens is closer, clearer
delete the eyes   vision will sharpen the glass along the way
with delicate lines engrave a bird
like one that was shattered as you watched
crumpled   discarded   on a manuscript rotting in a corner
your final death is intimately familiar with
an old room from which the wreckage of death waits to be removed

残忍的孩子

孩子们围绕一滴母亲的血跳舞
他们雪白的胳膊天生会抽打
四周疲倦的眼睛

第一颗牙齿　种在粉红色的田野里
当一只低垂的核桃被嗑开
他们看着母亲抽搐的脸　笑

笑着　在天空戏水
弯曲着　在丧失睡眠的黑夜镀银
孩子不睡时　世界也得醒着

在被抓破的长长的伤口上疯狂滑雪
聆听　最新的口令
这河水越透明　哭泣越清晰可见

仇恨　越像还没成形的肉一样流出
一支血污的口红　再也洗不掉
孩子跳舞

而母亲们被穿在脚上
像受宠的玩具　有足够的理由被毁灭
像好吃的手　不怕累地拉近未来

当他们用酷似死亡的宁静惊吓太阳
天使和苍蝇　都在鼓掌
一粒豆子　熟知怎样关上最后的门

CRUEL CHILDREN

the children dance around a drop of their mother's blood
snow-white arms born to thrash
the weary eyes all around them

with that first tooth   planted in the pink field
as mother cracks a hanging walnut
they watch her twisted face   and laugh

laugh   as they splash in the sky
wandering   the silvered nights of lost sleep
when children don't sleep   the world must wake up too

skiing madly down long scratched-open wounds
they listen to the latest commands
the more transparent this river   the more clearly are the tears seen

the more hatred   flows like as yet unformed flesh
bloodstain lipstick   can never be washed away
the children dance

their mother worn on their feet
like a favourite toy   with many reasons for its destruction
like a tasty hand   tirelessly hauling the future in

they frighten the sun with a horribly deathlike stillness
flies and angels   clap their hands
a little bean   knows how to close the final door

这个下午的花园

这个下午从来都是那个下午
长着蝙蝠脸的花朵　笑得更开心了
医院的窗户　像死者瞪出的眼白

碎片似的下午
花香在周围人家做客

烟囱中飞舞而出的灰烬　更鲜艳了
露出假牙的天使
捂住年龄像捂住狂风戏弄的裙子
一笑一个残忍的春天
再笑　笑声把花园提升到空中
不是虚幻的就无从诞生

靠伤口活着的人们嗅出了
伤口　被雨水浸湿　绽开　溢出香气

一个花园拥有所有的下午
被纸花插满的肉体　纸是唯一的装束
骨头灿烂　乌黑的枝头涌出骨朵
在死者深处孕育成花瓣
皮肤下蚯蚓横行
这寂静又甜又腥　从来都是
根　把心里的泥土抓碎后的那片寂静

当每一座医院都被花园包扎成礼品
伤口在阳光下多么鲜明多么茂盛

多像真的
蝉依旧喝血　依旧
从一枚空壳里杜撰没有心跳的笑声
更开心的花园四散各处

在蝙蝠们的尖叫中渐渐溶解
一下午的幽香卷走世界
连伤口都留不下　只剩臃肿的月亮还是
肉色的　还在看护一个完整的黑夜

THE GARDEN THIS AFTERNOON

this afternoon is always that afternoon
flowers growing bat-faced   smiling still more happily
hospital windows   like the white staring eyes of the dead

afternoon like a fragment
the perfume of flowers is all around everyone, visiting

ash floats from the chimney   more dazzling still
an angel showing false teeth
holding down age like holding down a skirt teased by the gale
each laugh a cruel springtime
another laugh   laughter lifts the garden into the air
what's not invented has no way of being born

those who depend on wounds have smelt
wounds   soaked by rain   split open   spill out perfume

a garden embraces all afternoons
flesh stuck full of paper flowers   paper is the only attire
bones magnificent   crow-black branches gush with buds
conceived as petals in the deep place of the dead
worms rampage beneath the skin
the silence is sweet and rank   is always
roots   that silence after the heart's soil has been raked apart

as every hospital is gift-wrapped by a garden
how bright, how luxuriant are wounds in sunlight

how like the real thing
cicadas drink blood as always   as always
fabricate from an empty shell a laughter with no heartbeat
the still-happier garden is scattered everywhere

dissolving among the shrill cries of bats
the still, secret perfume of the entire afternoon folds the world away
even wounds can't stay   there only remains the obese moon
flesh-coloured   still nursing an unbroken   night

母亲

如果梦见你的脸　你就再次诞生
轮回　这棵肉质的孱弱的树
早该坠满了果实

如果沙滩上你光着脚
雪白的盐粒　从浮肿的脚踝朝肩头爬
像你曾爬进一条早晨的隧道
鞋脱在门外
用一对聋耳忽略孤儿的呼喊

死亡　才是我们新的家庭
每年的烛光下　死者都成为女性的
你在隔壁的房间里更衣
像童年那样　不在乎衬裤中的细节
离开我　也离开一个世界的耻辱

而我被谁领进这梦里　参观一场病
血液在学校里笨拙描写的　只是你的病
你停在你死去的地点　让我追赶
追上你的年龄

隔着玻璃仿佛隔着一滴干透了的奶
我从你一瞥中目睹自己在变形
一场雨后　躯体都是别处
你一直站在那里
我却越来越远地死于缩小的距离
在一场梦或一个末日与你会合

恐怖的地基

地基以食肉的贪婪向上挖掘
它埋在地下的呼吸　同时埋在天空中
被岩石的乳头压死的孩子
骨骼裂开　像零零散散的星星
在一场风暴后苍白闪烁
瘫痪的躯体内　惟有仇恨能再生

MOTHER

if I see your face in a dream   then you are born again
reincarnate   this frail fleshly tree
should long ago have been bent heavy with fruit

if you go barefoot on a beach
snow-white grains of salt   climb from your swollen ankles to your
shoulders
so you climbed the tunnel of a morning
your shoes left outside the door
to neglect the orphans' cries with deaf ears

death   is our new household now
in the candlelight of every year   the dead become female
you change your clothes in the next room
as in childhood   oblivious to the details in the underwear
leaving me   and leaving a world's shame

but who leads me into this dream?   visiting a bout of sickness
blood clumsily portrayed in the classroom   it was only your sickness
you stay in the place where you died   making me run after you
to catch up with your age

cut off by glass, like being cut off by a drop of dried milk
in your one swift glance I saw myself changing shape
after a shower of rain   bodies are all elsewhere
you have stood there all along
but I die ever further away, across a shrinking divide
forgathering with you in a dream or at my final hour

THE FOUNDATIONS OF TERROR

with carnivorous greed terror digs upwards
the breath it buried below ground   simultaneously buried in the sky
a child smothered by a teat of stone
skeleton split open   like scattered stars
pallidly glittering after a storm
in a paralysed body   only hatred can be reborn

再活一次　把丑陋的器官
在春天的狂轰滥炸下再暴露一次
蓝图　浸进血污
冲洗我们废墟的第一张航空照片
我们毁灭　而你出现

你们毁灭　而他出现

他们毁灭　我们蹲在墙根下挖掘
一千个黄昏以钟表的精确缔造下一个
孩子　从天空的产床上挖出父母时
每个人为纪念自己的消失而诞生了

活　石头活着还得继续
在它里面坍塌　一个秘密战斗的战士
用下肢拥抱着他的马
一遍遍从绿草的屋顶上驰过
听到身后　大地像海面一样愈合
那被压死的孩子早已上千岁
早已变蓝　在笼罩生日的浓雾中行走

用我们的肉体　死亡
建造起从下面覆盖世界的村庄

读《地狱之门》

语言　从不是让人懂　只是被人说的
就像你躺在一个夜晚凝视自己的手
手指说　堕落的肉体优美的肉体
仍在石头瀑布上百年流动
长满铜锈的粉红色四肢
被波涛葬送时还在死死纠缠
被你可怕的思想　一一温柔抚摸
月光　像一件等待完成的杰作
把眼睛关在门外　而听觉是水
水底是一个暴露出人类愚蠢的机会

live again   take the ugly organs
and expose them again to the saturation bombing of spring
blueprints   soak into the bloodstains
develop the first aerial photo of our ruins
we are destroyed   and you appear

you are all destroyed   and he appears

they are all destroyed   we squat at the foot of the wall, digging
with the precision of a timepiece a thousand gloamings create the next
child   when parents are dug out of the childbed of the sky
everyone is born to commemorate their own disappearance

live   living stones still must carry on
collapsing inside   warrior in a secret battle
thighs embracing his horse
time and again galloping the length of the rooftops of green grass
behind him listening to   earth healing like the surface of the sea
that smothered child already a thousand years old
long ago turned blue   walking in the dense fog that shrouds birthdays

with our bodies   death
builds up a village which covers the world from below

READING "THE GATES OF HELL"

language   through not being understood   is only spoken
like you lying one night staring at your hand
the fingers said   degenerate flesh, exquisite flesh
still flowing for a century over waterfalls of stone
pink limbs all tarnished
while buried by huge waves, still horribly entangled
one by one softly stroked by your terrible thoughts
moonlight   like a masterpiece waiting to be finished
locks the eyes out   and hearing is water
below the water is a chance to expose human stupidity

你不是我们　你是那不能再沉溺的
青铜冷却的一刹那
从我们嘴里挖走最后的呼声
你在我们深处坐下　修饰每一块骨头

再呕吐出来　像漂满肿胀尸首的山洪
紧紧追逐一支手　整座雕塑上只有
这支手　说出每个人疯狂的流向
创造地狱的　决不是上帝——是鬼魂

这片埋葬凡·高的天空

生前挖掘墓穴的　只有艺术家和皇帝
一张画把世界变成了自己的影子
包括你　和你临终的抽搐
没人能活着步入这天空　除非埋进
一块死孔雀胸前妄想的蓝
被一颗发疯的花白头颅所照耀
肿瘤似的星座　把你垂直吸上去
你的死亡是最后暴露的金黄色
涂满了躯体　那小小的房间
当耻辱　一笔一笔写尽　天空诞生了

我们的声音只是另一把剃刀
割　每只企图聆听你寂静的耳朵
星是一群不流血的动物
激怒你　使你纯粹从天上轻蔑这人类

在死后　继续创造生者的空白
蓝色固定的大海　像一件孤独的工作
你　在画面上变硬　那把骨头
被黑夜烤干　谁也不知道地撒在到处

you are not us   you are that never-again drownable
bronze-cool instant
digging away the last cries from our mouths
you sit in our depths   embellishing every bone

vomit again   like a mountain torrent bobbing with swollen corpses
closely pursuing a hand   in the whole sculpture there is only
this hand   which tells the direction all men crazily drift toward
the creator of hell   isn't God, for sure — but a ghost

THIS SKY THAT BURIED VAN GOGH

only artists and emperors   dig their graves before they die
a painting turns the world into their own shadows
including you   and your deathbed twitching
no living man can step into the sky   unless buried in
the wishful blue of a dead peacock's breast
lit up by an insane grey skull
a tumour-like constellation   sucks you upright
your death the last golden yellow to be disclosed
smeared all over your body   that tiny room
as humiliation   is brushstroke by brushstroke written out   the sky
                                                                    is born
our voices are only a razor
severing   every ear that seeks to hear your silence
the stars are a flock of unbleeding beasts
enraging you   giving you a pure heavenly scorn for these humans

after death   you go on creating a void in the living
the blue static sea   like a single lonely piece of work
you   stiffen on the painting's surface   those bones
baked dry by night   scattered all around unnoticed

死于幻象的人

死于幻象的人　正如诗人死于一首诗
夏季进入你的塔于是高高在上
你像神一样思想神一样疯狂
每隔千年重新计算一群天鹅　修改
月亮　那黑瘦爪子下流血的秩序
用一种想象摆布一只老鼠时
你厌倦过　在智慧中死去仍然是死
可文字　第二次失传的石头艺术
嚼着你的肉发出腐臭
你又自己投入火　如一页报废的作品

这样　我们死于你
唯一传世的是一把大理石椅子
让你在瞎子的嚎哭中就坐
用一个人的脚　踩碎无辜的葡萄

幻象　你说　就是模仿幽灵去生活
去追问　像个年老的乞丐
死在街头　被野猫暗红的牙齿追悼
而一首诗炼成玫瑰　从来是骇人的奇迹

卡夫卡纪念馆

假如时间只是祖先们的作品　我们
早就用一声咳嗽不朽了

吐痰　意味着永恒　那再吐一口
就是纪念　我们判决
他必须活着　扮演一个被追捕的鬼魂

布拉格要在每一座雕花窗台上
展览这具挖出来暴晒的小小鼠尸
惨白精细的骨架
爪子把头抱得再紧　也躲不开阳光

Someone Who Dies in a Vision

someone who dies in a vision   is like a poet who dies in a poem
summer enters your tower and climbs
you meditate like a god, go mad like a god
obsessively count a flock of swans each millennium   amend
the moon   when an order bleeding from thin black claws
ingeniously manipulates a rat
you weary of it all   even with wisdom, dying is still death
but writing   that twice-lost stony art
reeks of rot as it gnaws on your flesh
you throw yourself into the flames again   like a work discarded

so   we die in you
the only inheritance a marble chair
your seat amid the keening of the blind
one man's feet   trampling the guiltless grapes

a vision   you said   that lives by imitating ghosts
to make inquiries   like an old beggar
dead on the street   mourned by the crimson teeth of wild cats
but a poem forged into a rose   is always astounding, a marvel

The Kafka Museum

if time is just an artefact of our ancestors'   then we
were long ago immortalised with a cough

hawking phlegm   signifying eternity   that second hawk
is commemoration   our verdict is
he must be alive   playing a captured ghost

on every carved windowsill   Prague
displays this dead mouse dug out to dry
pale, delicate skeleton
claws embracing head ever more tightly   unable to dodge the sun

逃进坟墓里　也是继续听
父亲们的石像在夜深时高声谈笑
妹妹们争吵　情人姗姗来迟
他必须懂得　怯懦　给我们权力

玩一副纸牌　让令他怕的轻蔑的世界
再次围观他的无能

加入一片自己憎恶的景色也能止疼
比被烧掉　更加止疼
我们看见他在鲜花里　在桥上
已经朗读了一百年
还将再朗读一百年
像被抽着　与每张油腻的脸合影
我们高兴　就索取一个被害者的签名

　　"卡夫卡"

梦中的高度

你不记得那个梦了　只有那高度
让你肉体中的肉体继续颤抖
鸟在最静时濒临某种危险
像月光的锤击下
花园麻木地嗅着自己
一地摔碎的银子依然头晕目眩
你不记得　可梦中那人
被一根肋骨挑上天空
还在那儿行走如摇摇欲坠的音乐

一个梦有时比一生更漫长
有时只是峭壁　让你用另一种年龄
衰老　黑暗的年龄——
如果黑暗不得不把你接住

escape into the tomb   and you must still go on hearing
stone statues of fathers talking loudly at dead of night
sisters squabbling   lovers limping in late
he must understand   the timid heart   gives us power

toy with a pack of cards   let the contemptuous world that frightened him
encircle him again to watch his incapacity

joining in a scene of self-loathing can also kill the pain
kills pain better   than being burned away
we see him among flowers   on a bridge
for a century he has been read aloud
will continue to be read aloud for another century
as if whipped into   joining a group photo with every greasy face
we are pleased   and demand the victim's signature

"Kafka"

DREAM HEIGHT

you don't remember the dream   only the height
makes the flesh in your flesh go on trembling
birds at the quietest of times are in imminent danger
under the beating of moonlight's hammer
the garden numbly sniffs at itself
on the floor shattered silver, as dizzy as ever
you don't remember   but the man in the dream
was raised by the rib into the sky
and like unsteady music walks there still

sometimes a dream is more drawn out than a life
sometimes it's just a precipice   ageing you
with different years   dark years—
if darkness must support you

生还

季节的花瓶时而拥挤时而空旷
但都是残缺的
一块碎玻璃仿刀的艺术
却暗自羡慕尸体能腐烂
就不必返回　像野猫毛色上的春天
一滴碧绿的血脏得像油
就让树木的枯骨发情
让我们忘记
生平唯一只尝试过纸上的死亡
比睡眠还短促的一夜
风用敌人的方式暗中走动
当月亮无非一个错字
上升　照耀　又淹没在墨水下面
我们直接从纸上跌入这早晨
像一次生还似的学习去死

事

你还是那样　安静地走出一件事
许多件中的一件
许多荒废岁月中的一天
当腐烂的田野再次脱下你的鞋子
雪　用冻红的脚趾支撑你

这个日子天空灰暗却没有雪意
只有你的寒冷从生到死
往事无声　雪上留不下脚印

旧衣服总是谦虚的　像死者的木床
从另一对性交的肉体下滑向海洋
一件往事里再不能发生别的事
一生的错误　站成山上耸立的树
比雪更远的白
那骨头走出你
日子走出骨头　你们
被互相丢在身后

互相看着许多空无一人的月光

SURVIVORS

the vases of the seasons are now dense, now sparse
but all are incomplete
a piece of broken glass imitates the knife's art
yet secretly envies the corpse that can rot
and not have to return   like spring on a wild cat's coat
a drop of dark green blood stains like oil
makes the trees' dry bones come on heat
makes us forget
that death on paper, the only one we've tried in this life
a night briefer yet than sleep
the wind moves secretly in enemy form
as the moon, no more than a misprint
rises   shines   drowns under ink again
we tumble into this morning straight off the paper
as if we are survivors learning how to die

INCIDENT

you're still that way   calmly walking away from an incident
one incident among so many
one day among so many neglected months and years
as rotten fields remove your shoes once again
snow   sustains you on frostbitten toes

the day's overcast, grey, but doesn't look like snow
only your coldness moves from life towards death
past events are silent   can't leave footprints in the snow

old clothes are always modest   just the way the wooden cots of the dead
slip to the sea from below another pair of bodies making love
no other incident can happen in a past one
a lifetime of mistakes   stand like towering trees on a mountain
more distantly white than snow
that bone walks out of you
the days walk out of the bone   you
are thrown away, one behind the other

seeing each other as so many uninhabited moonbeams

医院

盖子合拢　你脸上是否也钉满了钉子
像一生的耻辱那么多唾沫
早已漂白了这轻而易举的死亡

一只手摸不到自己的疼痛
这个夜晚的黑暗　全都置身事外
你租用薄薄的四壁

在一只纸盒中聆听一条河流
在空出来的骸骨间　聆听暴风雨
等候下一位病人

像另一滴泪水飞进你眼里
一声尖叫　撞到白花花的玻璃上
变成欢呼　你在狠狠钉着钉子

死地

你需要　墙上除了黎明什么都没有
花园是内心的倒影　永远在离开
你需要那些眼睛盯着
你　选出最容易被忘记的一双
开始忘记

怕　你怕每天长着麻雀脸的寂静
暴力从四点延续到六点
音乐剩下一把被剔净的骨头
在田野上敲打
没人知道你此刻是否耳鸣

你也不知道　只需要房间空着
用一生学会对自己无情
用阳光窥视一个从未得到的真的末日
除了阳光什么都不是眼泪
花园的名字　还没出口已被忘记

76

HOSPITAL

the lid closes   whether or not your face is hammered full of nails
spittle, as much as in a lifetime of humiliation,
long since bleached out this light, easy death

a hand can't reach its own pain
the darkness of this night   stands altogether outside events
you rent four flimsy walls

listen to the river flowing inside a paper carton
between bones left blank   listen to the storm
wait for the next patient

as another tear flies into your eye
a shrill shout   collides with the shining glass
becomes a cheer   you're ruthlessly driving the nails in

DEATHTRAP

you need   apart from the dawn there's nothing on the wall
the forever-departing garden a reflection of your inmost heart
you need those eyes staring at
you   choose the ones easiest to forget
start forgetting

fear   you fear the daily sparrow-faced silence
violence continues from four o'clock to six
music leaves behind a bone scraped clean
knocking on the fields
no-one knows if your ears are ringing at this moment

you don't know either   just need the emptiness of the room
use a lifetime to learn to be heartless with yourself
use the sunlight to spy on a real but never-attained dying day
apart from the sunlight nothing is tears
the garden's name   is forgotten before it's spoken

山谷

当我们抵达黑暗时　在谷底见到光
岩石　深邃如天空
如一架危险的楼梯突然折断
胆怯的手指弯向狂暴的星群哭泣
把我们弄成残废的
还是欺骗我们的双眼

当光成为一种生物时　我们是死的
那些蠕动的小小肉体
在我们身上钻孔　照耀
月亮像一个人摊开四肢坠落
城市躺在错觉丛生的床上
阅读一本阴暗的书　封面是大海
封底　是野兽践踏着泥水的蹄声
陷阱　想起时总在脚下

当距离消失　我们才摸到鲜红的溪流
用石头的皱纹　展览出从前所有的恐惧

恨的履历

黄昏时每一次散步都不是走向别人
火　再也无从被照亮
像仇恨　斟满自己的杯子
让我痛饮
一棵果树里那么甜的血
一个被白昼染得更黑的黑夜
四肢松开　风暴像舌头般摇撼
眼睛留在昨天的宽阔病房里
是一件会射击的乐器
鸟不属于现实　因而总在逃离
一片与玻璃相混淆的目光
最清澈的水依然是瞎子
住在鲨鱼寂静心中的人只能干裂
看着大海把自己烧完

Mountain Valley

as we come to darkness   on the valley floor we see light
rocks   deep as the sky
suddenly snap like a dangerous staircase
timid fingers bent toward the violent stars weep
what turns us into cripples
is our own eyes, deceived by looking

as light becomes a creature   we are dead
these tiny squirming bodies
drill holes into us   shining
moonlike a spreadeagled falling man
a city lying on a bed overgrown with illusion
reading a dark book   its cover the ocean
its back   the sound of wild animals' hooves on mud
pitfalls   when you think of it, are always underfoot

as distance has vanished   we touch a bright red rivulet
wrinkled with stones   exhibiting every terror that ever was

CV of Hate

no twilight stroll ever leads to anyone else
fire   can never be lit once again
like hatred   filling its own cup full
making me drink madly drink my fill
blood so sweet within a fruit tree
a black night dyed blacker by the daylight
limbs slacken   storm shakes violent as a tongue
the eyes left in yesterday's broad sickroom
are a musical instrument that shoots
birds belong to no reality   so their flight is unending
gaze indistinguishable from glass
clearest of water is a still blind man
who lives in the shark's silent heart, parched, can only split open
seeing the ocean burn itself up

看着珊瑚　剔净胸前多余的肉
擦亮死亡像一件小小的饰物
装饰死后的岁月
——恨我吧　因为我还渴

从我窗口望出去的街道

从我窗口望出去的街道总是不下雨
它镇静得像一把梳子
搁在窗台上
它在等待　一个不声不响的女人
像只累了的海鸥从海边飞来
像粒石子两手抱紧自己
她背上　翻毛的灰色口袋里
一只柠檬在悄悄改变形状

从我窗口望出去的街道白雪皑皑
整个冬天　街上只有
七只野猫和一个睡破汽车的男人
或者八双一模一样的眼睛
像被打空的麦粒毫无怨意
他们亲热得使我相信
他们已许下互相用尸体充饥的诺言
和犹如保证的　最温柔地抚摸

与星同游

在逃难的地平线两边　星星是和你
同步的水晶风暴
半个天空像被收割后的田野
你是一粒小麦　在磨坊里磨着
你眺望　像仇敌们互相思念
一个人用星的步子行走百年
在那海边喝水
听那鼓声　从前额敲击到脑后

80

seeing the corals   scrape their breasts clean of surplus flesh
polish death bright like a tiny little ornament
decorate the months and the years after death
—hate me, then   because I'm still thirsty

THE STREET I SEE FROM MY WINDOW

on the street I see from my window it never rains
it lies by my windowsill
composed and calm as a comb
waiting   for a silent woman
flying in from shore like a tired seagull
hands hugging herself as tight as a pebble
on her back   in a furry grey satchel
a lemon quietly changing shape

the street I see from my window is white with snow
all winter   on the street only
seven stray cats and a man sleeping in an abandoned car
or eight identical pairs of eyes
empty corn husks, utterly free of resentment
so affectionate I am convinced
they have promised to feed each other with their corpses
and, like a guarantee   the gentlest of touching

TRAVELLING WITH THE STARS

at either end of the refugee horizon   the stars
a crystal tempest in time with you
half the sky like harvested fields
you are a grain of wheat   grinding in the mill
you scan the scene   the way that enemies yearn for each other
a man walking through a century in time with the stars
drinking water on that seashore
hearing that drum   beating from the forehead to the back of the brain

刺破皮肤　把骨头凿刻得根根银白
看着星星自己也浮动起来
你在你里边浮动
时差　随着一具躯体而腐烂
金色大海随着星光才暴露食肉的过程
半个天空　残存活着的深度
落下
你是被选中的另外半个
在不得不明亮时不得不四分五裂

血橙

女孩子藏在薄薄的皮肤下
走投无路的血　在等待一个伤口
躯体被切掉一半时　会哭叫

像一只游入暗红水池的青蛙
裸露的肉总有某种甜味儿
让你用嘴唇猜测她的心跳

吸干　那小小子宫里
滴滴渗出来不及擦去的贪婪的果子
麻雀抖动　白色的鸟粪坠落枝头

落到你牙上　无动于衷地吐核
忘记　再次撕开一个微笑
你湿润的喉咙里流的是脓

黎明之前

蝴蝶的铁翅膀　刨子一样经过
宁静的花蕊总是剧毒的
水闸提起来　白内障患者的眼里
世界是一篇苍茫的译文

stabbing skin   chiselling bones one by one into silvery white
looking at the stars you too begin to float
floating inside yourself
time differences   decaying along with the body
only following starlight does the gold ocean disclose its flesh-eating
                                                                    processes
half the sky   remains the depth of life
falls
you are the other half that is chosen
when you can't help shining you can't help falling apart

BLOOD ORANGE

girls conceal beneath flimsy skin
flowing blood with no outlet   waiting for a wound
a body, when it's sliced in half   can weep, cry out

like a frog swimming in a dark red pond
exposed flesh always has a kind of sweetness
lets your lips guess at her heartbeat

suck it dry   from that tiny womb
leaks out, drop by drop, greedy fruit it's too late to wipe away
sparrows tremble   white birdshit falls from branches

lands on your teeth   nonchalantly spit the pips out
forget   tear open a smile once again
what flows in your moistened throat is pus

BEFORE DAYBREAK

iron wings of butterflies   pass like spokeshaves
tranquil stamens are always deadly poison
sluice gates start lifting   in the eyes of cataract sufferers
the world is a vague translation

背对窗口　一个人制作他自己的恶梦
用黑暗的字喂饱关在身体里的野兽
木匠的手拎着滴血的斧头
寻找女人两腿间那一窝臭虫

抽去骨头的细节　使描写更加完美
当嗅觉裹着一层皮睡熟
呼喊　也像死在开水中的盐
能挤过这道窄门的　只有扁平的鬼魂

牛

值得向往的艺术是静静站立的艺术
绿色总是比你醒得更早
草屑　沾满圆圆的肚子　像一片
沿着黑暗肩胛迅速揭开的黎明

没有牛　就不会有田野
没有田野　童年的谎言又怎能
继续迷人　继续让你喝一杯每天的奶

用黑和白的金子打造小小的神龛
犁沟埋下蹄印　像一种疼痛的预感
牛的躯体被你目光肢解时
变成真的　剥去皮只剩血淋淋的桃子
无肉的骨头　草原上完美的雕塑
活的黄昏袒露出死亡

而　内心的冲撞里　月亮才升起

back to the window   a man creates his own nightmares
with words made of darkness he feeds the beasts locked in his body
the carpenter's hand carries a bloody axe
to seek out that nest of bedbugs between a woman's thighs

boneless details   make description still more perfect
when the sense of smell, wrapped in skin, falls sound asleep
cries   are like salt dead in boiling water
no-one can squeeze through this narrow gate   except flat ghosts

Cow

an art worth waiting for is the art of standing still
green always wakes earlier than you do
wisps of grass   stick to the round stomach   like
daybreak swiftly uncovered along the shoulder of the dark

no cow   so there can't be any fields
no fields   and how can the lies of childhood
still be charming   still let you drink your daily milk

with white and dark gold forge a tiny altar
furrows bury hoofprints   like painful foreknowledge
when your sight dismembers the cow's body
it becomes real   once flayed it becomes a bloody peach
fleshless bones   flawless sculpture on the grasslands
living dusk exposing death

but   in a collision of the heart   the moon rises

绝对的问题

你在浴室中想到一个绝对的问题
谁能把风吹进水面

像光　潜泳的雪白的双腿
蚕在一只眼睛里吐丝

沙子　从玻璃的指缝间漏下
皮肤失去孤寂就大声哭泣

蜘蛛使你的性闪闪发光时
候鸟们由于飞行而改变了生日

水下此刻　风向偏北
邪恶　是沉默中进入秘密的知识

夏季的惟一港口
——给友友

天空更加阴暗　你说　这船老了
一生运载的风暴都已走远
该卸下自己了　让石头船舷去腐烂
夏季　是惟一的港口

夜晚　发红的锈蚀的古老铁环
早就断了　你说　月亮像被弃的婴儿
在水上写字的人只能化身为水
把港口　变成伤口

听　炎热雨声里那不变的记忆
雨到处刺痛你　雨声是最后的小屋
让你居住　你老了　船说

这惟一一个夏季漂泊了多年
惟一一个时间　注入漆成黑色的家
波浪之下只有我们的躯体

ABSOLUTE QUESTION

in the bathroom you thought of an absolute question
who can blow a wind into the water's surface?

like the light   snow-white thighs swimming underwater
silkworms spinning silk in an eye

grains of sand   leak from between the glass's fingers
skin loses its loneliness and weeps aloud

when a spider makes your sex shine bright
because of their flight migrant birds change their birthdays

in this moment underwater   the wind turns to the north
evil   is the knowledge that enters secrets in silence

SUMMER'S ONE AND ONLY HARBOUR
for Youyou

the sky was even darker   you said   this boat's ageing
the storms it carried for a lifetime are all gone
it should unload itself   let its stone sides rot
summer   is the only harbour

night   an ancient hoop of iron reddening and corroding
long broken   you said   the moon's like an abandoned infant
those who write on water must be embodies as water
turn a harbour   to a wound

listen   to the unchanging memory in the blazing sound of rain
rain lacerates you   its sound is the final tiny room
you live in   you're ageing   the boat said

this, the one and only summer, has been drifting for years
the one and only time   flowing into a house painted black
below the waves, there are only our bodies

无人称的雪（之一）

一场雪干燥　急促　模仿一个人的激情
兽性的昏暗白昼
雪用细小的爪子在树梢上行走

细小的骨骼
一场大火提炼的玻璃的骨骼

雪　总是停在
它依然刺耳的时候

关于死　死者又能回忆起什么
一具躯体中秘密洒满了银子
一千个孕妇在天上分娩
未经允许的寒冷孤儿
肉的淡红色梯子　通向小小的阁楼
存放尸首的　白色夜晚的阁楼

你不存在　因而你终年积雪

无人称的雪（之二）

西尔斯　马利亚

雪地上布满了盲人　他们看不见
一首死人在旅馆里的诗
和　繁殖着可怕阳光的山谷

他们在同一座悬崖下失去了影子
变成花园日规上黑瘦的针
用笑声洗脚

用一只死鸟精心制作雕花的器皿
野餐时痛饮鲜红的溪流
正午　盲人盲目分泌的溪

他们看不见　一首诗里的游客
都裸体躺在旅馆的床上
无须陷落　就抵达一场雪崩的深度

The Non-Personal Snow 1

the snowfall is arid   rushed   imitates human enthusiasm
a brutish, dusky daylight
snow walks along the treetops with tiny claws

tiny skeletons
skeletons of glass refined by fierce fire

snow   always stops
the moment it's still grating on the ear

as for death   what can the dead still remember?
a body secretly sprinkled all silver
a thousand pregnant women giving birth in the sky
cold orphans still not given permission
a pink ladder of flesh   leads to a tiny attic
a tiny attic of white night   where corpses are kept

you don't exist   so all year round you are snow-capped

The Non-Personal Snow 2
Sils-Maria, Switzerland

the snowy ground is covered with blind men   they can't see
the poem that died in the hotel
and   the valleys that breed the fearsome sunlight

below the same precipices they lose their shadows
become thin black needles on the garden sundial
wash their feet in laughter

take pains to carve patterned vessels from a dead bird
drink deep at picnic time of the scarlet stream
noon   the scarlet stream exuded by blind eyes

they can't see   the tourists in the poem
lying naked in hotel beds
no need to fall   to get to the depths of an avalanche

无人称的雪（之三）

一盏陶土小灯　是你送给黑暗的礼物
雨声和雨声的摩擦中
诞生了你名字里的雪
给你纹身的雪
疼痛　放出关进岩石多年的鸟群
一只是一个辞　而你是无辞的
风暴　是城市屋顶上一座空中墓园
天使　也得在窝里舔伤
像头黄金的野兽蹲在昔日
被水显形的人不得不随水流去
一场大雪犹如下到死后的音乐
你在名字每天死后
袒露一具没人能抚摸的肉体
让天空摸
从雪到血　摸遍火焰
直至黑暗　偿还不知是谁的时间

无人称的雪（之四）
西尔斯　马利亚

黑夜像一个疯子的思想　敲打
我们的头颅　使我们相遇
危险的雪不存在距离
像两片星光下驰过同一座山峰的马
被一枚埋入夏夜的钉子扎着
听鬼魂们洒水　清扫月亮
听　墓碑说谎　炫耀人生的艺术

我们都是下山的　雪
天生无人称因而挥霍每个人的死亡
黑夜在病床上　挥霍妄想时
疯子们的村庄在弹琴
蜡烛不朽　钟声泼出眼泪
一副白骨漫山遍野脱下日子的丧服
而　我们冻结成一整块石头

THE NON-PERSONAL SNOW 3

a little clay lamp   is your present to darkness
in the clashing together of the sounds of the rain
the snow in your name is born
snow that tattoos your body
pain   releases flocks of birds shut up for years in stones
each one a word   and you are wordless
the storm   is a cemetery in the air above city roofs
angels too   in the nest must lick their wounds
like a golden beastkneeling on the old days
a person revealed by water just has to follow the current
a snowfall is like music that goes down to death
you, when a name dies every day
expose a body that no-one can caress
let the sky feel
from snow to blood   feel all over the flame
until darkness   pays back some unknown person's time

THE NON-PERSONAL SNOW 4
Sils-Maria, Switzerland

night like a madman's thoughts   knocks
on our skulls   making us encounter
dangerous snow from a non-existent distance
like horses racing past a single peak beneath two stars
with the pricking of a nail buried in the summer night
hear ghosts laying the dust   sweeping the moon
hear   headstones tell lies   flaunt the arts of living

we are all slipping downhill   snow
innately non-personal and so squandering each person's death
night on the sickbed   squanders vain hopes
as the village of madmen strums on
candles are undying   bells sprinkle tears
on mountains and in fields white bones take off the mourning dress of
                                                        our days

and   we are frozen into one entire stone

无人称的雪（之五）

这山谷不可登临
一如你里面　那座白色夜晚的阁楼

被雪邀请时　花草一片寂静
视野　像一杯斟入黑暗的酒
在不同地点燃烧

被雪拒绝时　你是无色的
栖息在伤口里的鹰　用阳光小声哭泣
岩石　慢慢吞下你
而你的性闪耀你死后不可能的亮度

你成为唯一的不可能时
一生的雪都落下了

白色夜晚的阁楼里　钳子在夹紧
鸟儿脆弱的睡梦里　天空无情欢呼
女孩胸前甜蜜的梨子　掉进
雨季　雨声　就在你里面到处追逐你
一个人赤裸到最后无非一片雪

在山谷脚下洁白　刺眼

走了千年还没穿过这间没有你的房子

无人称的雪（之六）
西尔斯　马利亚

只活在时间里的人知道时间并非时间
一块岩石本身就是一首诗
而阴影　镌刻成一把湖边的椅子
每年六月的野草　在这儿朗读
雪　死者银白的书
那铁丝棕毛的刷子仍固执刷着

The Non-Personal Snow 5

this mountain valley can't be visited
just like inside you   that attic of white night

when you're invited by the snow   flowers and plants are a silence
field of vision   like a glass of wine poured into darkness
burning in other places

when you're turned down by the snow   you are colourless
a hawk roosting in a wound   softly weeping sunlight
rock   slowly swallows you
and your sex shines with a brilliance impossible after death

when you have become the only impossibility
a lifetime's snows have already fallen

in the attic of white night   forceps tightly pinch
in the fragile dreams of birds   the sky cheers heartlessly
sweet pears on girls' breasts   fall into
the rainy season   the sound of rain   chases you all over your insides
an utterly naked person is nothing but a field of snow

spotless white underfoot in the valley   glaring

a walk of a thousand years still hasn't crossed this room you aren't in

The Non-Personal Snow 6

Sils-Maria, Switzerland

those who live in time know time isn't time
a rock is itself a poem
and shadow   engraved as a seat by a lake
weeds every June   read aloud here
snow   the silver-white book of the dead
and the brush of steel wire and coir is still stubbornly sweeping

一双泥泞棺木的鞋子
一副纸手铐　更使囚犯胆战心惊
这一个个字　写下就错了
刻上悬崖的字　搭乘着失控的缆车
日复一日粉身碎骨
跳入一首诗的诗人只配粉身碎骨

比死亡更逼真的想象里
雪是一次漫步　仅仅一次
六月就齐声腐烂　死者的肉体摇着铃
所有人　摇着此刻完成的孤独的铃
比想象更逼真地死亡着
雪　离开太远了　不得不埋葬一切

a pair of muddy shoes of wooden coffin
a set of paper handcuffs   make the convict more terrified yet
these words   go wrong when written down
words carved on cliffs   ride on a runaway cable car
broken apart day after day
poets who leap into a poem deserve only to be broken apart

in an imagination more lifelike than death
snow is a once-only walk   once and once only
June rots in chorus   as the bodies of the dead ring bells
all men   are ringing solitary bells that are fulfilled in this moment
dying more lifelike than in imagination
snow   has gone too far   can't help burying everything

面具与鳄鱼

2. Masks and Crocodile

摘不掉的面具
——《面具与鳄鱼》序

我不知道这些诗是写在澳大利亚还是中国？

那天早上。在悉尼。一个靠海的房间。阳光骤然亮起。粼粼水波里，满墙面具活起来，用层层叠叠的眼睛看着我。

那许多早上。在北京。我的名为"鬼府"的小屋，像一块深埋在黄土下的化石，把成千上万年的岁月拥抱在怀里。那么多被遗忘的脸，曾经活过，如今却只在农民们世代流传的、雕刻辟邪脸谱的手艺里，萎缩成一个影子。一动不动地笑。大红大绿地哭叫。

高大的博物馆里，镀金画框囚禁着脸的漫长历史。古老的西安，沉重的土地掀开一角，被压碎的陶俑们，目瞪口呆地与生者面面相视。天安门广场上，下水道堵塞了，一堆堆血肉中是谁的耳朵、鼻子、嘴、。。。。。。它们看着我，比死亡更冷漠。我在它们眼里，比面具更虚幻。影子的影子，刚刚诞生却就已逝去。

我不知道我写了这些诗，还是没写？这些辞，神秘的中国字，每一个是一座老房子，四堵高墙内流失了数不清的时间。好像在水上，我侧耳倾听，身体里另一个人渐渐远去的脚步声。只有远去，却永无抵达。我开口说话，一页白纸上荡开不知是谁的回音。诗人和诗已这样对峙了千年。

或许诗从来是没有的。它只是一片寂静，像清晨群鸟歌唱时那么寂静。每一种语言因此诞生，因此以沉默为终极的光明：

> 万物是蓝
> 当我缺席时那么蓝

或许诗人只能从一个辞到另一个辞，一张面具到另一张面具，像隐身人一样永恒流浪，永远寻找，那等在某时某地的另一个自己。

我的脸也早已被挂在墙上。这些辞就是一堵墙。世界厌倦透了脱口而出或再三沉吟的死亡。每一秒钟里，我的脸越来越麻木，变成别人的脸。我的眼睛越来越空洞，听任蛆虫在里面挖掘墓穴，展开一场与生俱来的大屠杀。温情脉脉地，习惯对自己说谎。摆出一个姿势，对触目的罪恶视而不见。太久地沉溺于黑暗，我们与黑暗已融为一体。

那么，我们怎么能分辨：这块摘不掉的肮脏面具下，那不断更换的眼神是谁的？嗫嚅着同一话语的不同嗓音是谁的？当名字离开，一具具匿名的躯体是谁？当每天像一个死者，从我们身边倒下，一个个仍在呼吸的空白影子是谁？

是那么多被遗忘的脸，穿过时间回到我身上？还是我的脸如同这

THE MASK THAT CAN'T BE TAKEN OFF
— a Preface to *Masks and Crocodile*

I have no idea where I wrote these poems, in Australia? or in China?

That morning. Sydney. A house by the sea. the sun suddenly flared up and the water became crystalline. All the masks on the wall came back to life, looking at me with layers of eyes.

Many mornings. Beijing, the little room, which I named 'Ghost Mansions', was like a fossil deeply buried in the yellow soil, hugging hundreds of thousands of days and nights to its bosom. Those long-forgotten faces, though once alive, existed now only in the farmers' patrimony of apotropaic masks, shrinking into mere shadows, motionlessly laughing and colourfully crying.

In these great museums, gilded frames confined the long history of faces; in ancient Xi'an, one corner of the heavy earth was lifted up, and the smashed terracotta warriors faced the strangers with astonishment; in the grand square of Tiananmen, the sewers were choked up. In the mass of blood and flesh, these were ears, noses, mouths, all belonging to someone . . . They cast their eyes on me, more apathetic than the dead. I was no less illusory in their eyes than a mask, the shadow of shadows, a man newly-born yet long dead.

I don't know if I wrote these poems or not. These words, those mysterious Chinese characters, are each an ancient house within whose four-square high walls, countless eras have drained away. It seems that it was on the water, when I pricked up my ears attentively, the footsteps of someone else within my body gradually faded away, leaving but never reaching anywhere. I began to speak, but who knows whose voice echoed on the white paper. This has been thee confrontation of poet and poem for thousands of years.

Perhaps there is no such thing as poem at all. It is just a pool of quietness, like the silence, the silence made by singing birds in early morning. Every language is born in this, treating silence as its ultimate brightness:

> Everything is blue,
> So blue when I am absent.

Perhaps the poet can only move from one word to another, one mask to another, like an invisible person who lives in eternal rootless wandering,

些诗，被遗忘后，结识了它们并一起悄悄生长？

那么，到处都是这儿。这片刻已足够永恒。

或许悉尼者靠海的房间，已等了千年。死者都活着，所有影子停在身体里，一直像海一样波动。而北京我那间古老的小屋，从来只拥抱过一个时辰——当我认不出我的脸，我却认出了每一张脸；当所有辞远离，手中却留下一行诗。

那天早上，鸟叫时，很静。

seeking forever for the other possible self waiting in another time, and another place.

My face has long been hung as well. The words are the wall. The world has been weary of impulsive utterance or the prudent undertones of death. Every second, my face is becoming more numb and changing into that of the other. My eyes are becoming inane and empty, no longer feeling the maggots' mining of the tomb — a continual massacres long as I have lived. I have been used to lie to myself sentimentally and take the position of being blind to wickedness. Having been so long in the dark, we have become part of it.

Then how can we distinguish whose are the endlessly-changing eyes behind these dirty masks they can't take off? Whose are the different voices that murmur the same words? When their names have gone, who are those anonymous bodies? When every day falls down like a corpse, who are those blank shadows, still breathing beside us?

Are these long-forgotten faces returning to me through time? Or, does my face, after being forgotten like these poems, get to know them and quietly grow alongside them?

Everywhere is therefore here. And this one moment lasts an eternity.

Perhaps the house beside the sea in Sydney has been waiting for thousands of years. The dead are all alive with all the shadows that stop in my body like waves endlessly rippling in the sea. My ancient little room in Beijing, however, embraces only one moment — when I can't recognize my own face, I can recognize that of the others'; when all the words are gone, one line of poetry remains in my hand.

On that morning when the birds sang so quietly.

面具

一

面具自脸诞生
模拟脸
又忽略脸

面具　自空白之页诞生
掩饰空白
又只有空白

二

这个字有你的脸
精雕细刻
无表情地打磨了上千次

最后　被遗忘撕下
血淋淋摊开
你听见神呕吐的声音

三

脸无言崩溃
噩梦在肉里
一寸一寸把你凿空

海难后的船只
牙缝松弛
与烂泥混为一谈

四

你盯着那些脸嵌进木头
黝黑腐朽的眼角
木屑纷纷

MASKS

1

mask is born from a face
simulates the face
and elides the face

mask   born from an empty page
concealing the emptiness
again there's only emptiness

2

in this word is your face
lovingly carved
expressionlessly polished a thousand times

finally   torn away by forgetting
bloodily unfolded
you hear the gods throw up

3

face wordlessly collapses
nightmares in the flesh
gouge you out inch by inch

boats after danger on the sea
gaps between teeth widening
indistinguishable from slime

4

you're staring at these faces embedded in wood
corners of your eyes blackened and rotten
sawdust flying all over

盯着　脸和脸磕碰在
干裂的墙上
无视镜前的你

五

彩绘的脸犹如谎言中的字眼
一旦啐出　月光下
病人就成群梦游

一尾尾死鱼
诞生似地翻起
以空白　触摸黑暗

六

地貌可疑地起伏
在口音里
鸟类蹑足走近

春天说着呓语
再次暗转
绿与黄　含糊其辞

七

脸一直沉默
而你躲在它后面
说谎

脸也被说出
像同样惨遭欺骗的
谎言

staring   face knocking into face on
the cracked dry wall
unable to see the you who is before the mirror

5

coloured-in face like the wording of a lie
once spat out   then in moonlight
patients start sleepwalking

dead fish one by one
turned over like they're being born
through blankness   touching the dark

6

dubiously the land rises and falls
in its accent
birds tiptoe indoors

spring is talking in its sleep
more blackouts
green and yellow   equivocating

7

face silent all along
and you hide behind it
lying

face spoken out too
like the same cruelly cheated
lie

八

你用上千年临摹这片空白
画布似笑非笑
脸的古老托拓片

博物馆一样重写
历史仅仅一页
久已埋在你的书里失传

九

假面无须再被油漆遮掩
或胭脂
或黑布

沿街展览
薄施的笑容下
脸已逃之夭夭

十

在海里寻觅一滴水
就像在面具下
寻觅一个人

你听见他说话
听到血液
喝干肉体的声音

十一

鸟在空中的索道上滑行
陡然升起
像攀援一道绝壁

8

for thousands of years you copied this emptiness
canvas smile that is no smile
an ancient rubbing of a face

the museum over-written the same
history just a single page
long ago buried in your book and lost

9

no need to cover a false face with more paint
or rouge
or black cotton

on display along the street
below a thin smile
the face has cut and run

10

looking for a drop of water in the sea
like looking for someone
behind a mask

you listen to him speak
hear the sound of blood
drinking dry the flesh

11

bird slides on the high wire in the sky
ascending abruptly
like hauling yourself up a rock wall

一个字　读遍碧空
平衡着风
稍纵即逝

十二

遗忘里有许多丢失的面孔
层层叠叠　像蘑菇
簇拥着开口

或病或梦的白
以记忆为菌种
在每张脸下繁殖许多遗忘

十三

你把自己抵押给一个辞
抵押给一把刻刀
修饰得比寂静更哑默

辞在你嘴上横行
辞炫耀你的脸
挥霍赎不回的笑声

十四

往事静静吃木头
黄昏里这张脸
依旧在衰老

日渐密集的洞穴
每一只蛀虫
回了家　晚餐在暮色时辰

one syllable   reading over a cloudless sky
balancing with the wind
gone in a moment

12

there are lost faces in forgetting
layer upon layer   like mushrooms
huddling together to speak

the white of disease or dreams
memory its spores
breeds forgetting beneath every face

13

you pawn yourself for a word
pawned for an engraver's chisel
decorated dumber than silence

words run wild in your mouth
words flaunt your face
squander unredeemable laughter

14

the past is silently eating timber
this face in twilight
is aging as it always has

daily denser caves
every bookworm
gone home   dinner at the hour of dusk

十五

在时间里没有安宁
死亡里也没有
一张脸停顿的地方

海　泼妇般扭动
你眼巴巴瞪着礁石
你和它擦肩而过

十六

你大声向墙说话
你说出一堵墙
你被挂在墙上

墙到处走动
墙看着墙
墙对墙哑口无言

十七

这孤零零的牙齿目空一切
远离了脸
远离了说出口的声音

声音残缺不全
咀嚼过一切
比牙齿更像石头

十八

婴儿的腭骨细小而结实
被死亡摘下
学会无声地喋喋不休

15

no tranquillity in time
none in death either
the place where a face pauses

sea   twisting like a fishwife
you stare at the reef helplessly
you and it rubbing shoulders

16

you speak loudly to the wall
take the words out of the wall's mouth
you are hung on the wall

walls walking everywhere
walls watching walls
walls struck dumb by walls

17

this solitary tooth looks down on everything
far away from the face
far away from the sounds spoken from the mouth

the sounds are fragments
chewing everything up
more like stones than teeth

18

the baby's palate is tiny yet solid
taken off by death
it learns its noiseless unending chatter

几粒乳牙与生者
对视了多年
早已苍老得皱纹纵横

十九

你熟悉一张脸
和脸后面某种回声
深邃地传来

自白骨星座
黑暗中躲避你的瞳孔
走投无路的回声

二十

镜子抓不住脸
也抓不住凸凹不平的字
镜子背后没有世界

所以脸转过去
风平浪静
是另一张脸

二十一

墓碑石最后摘下的面具
放弃脸的人们
终于彼此认出

开始说同一种语言
耳朵烂掉时
海　洞穿头颅越响越清晰

milk teeth and the living
have watched each other for years
long ago so old they're criss-crossed by wrinkles

19

you're familiar with a face
and the echo behind that face
transmitted through profundity

from the constellation of white bones
your pupils hide you in darkness
an echo between a rock and a hard place

20

the mirror can't hold the face still
nor can if hold still the rough and uneven words
there's no world behind the mirror

so the face has turned around
wind and wave are calm and still
is another face

21

the gravestone is the last mask to be taken off
people who have abandoned their faces
recognise each other at last

begin to speak the same language
when the ears have rotted away
sea   pounds more loudly as it penetrates the skulls

二十二

死者从远处看城市
大理石眼睛
裹入鸟声

海择定这片墓园
让死者看见
大理石比脸更快地腐烂

二十三

霉菌在早晨悄悄滋长
潮湿的牙根
仍像生前窃窃私语

相视而笑
死亡给你洗脸
五官水一样流下

二十四

谎言杀害了说谎者
像脸杀死
追逐脸的人

而脸也被杀死
被谎言遗弃在墙上
咧开一道裂缝似的嘴唇

二十五

许多字在空白上展览
许多脸在素不相识中
遥远地冲撞

22

from far away the dead see the city
eyes of marble
sucked into birdsong

the sea has chosen this graveyard
to let the dead see
marble rots faster than faces

23

mould silently grows on the morning
moist roots of teeth
still like the soft whisper of a lifetime

smiling at one another
death washes your face for you
your features flowing down like water

24

lying has murdered the liar
like a face killing death
a person chasing a face

and the face killed too
forsaken on the wall by lying
lips widening in a rip-like grin

25

many words are displayed on blank space
many faces are unknown to one another
randomly colliding

彼此叠入
同一张脸素不相识
不同的字同时是空白

二十六

被活埋在脸深处的你
只能拼命诅咒
不间断的坏天气

眼角发了霉
爬满青苔的墓碑
在死者摸不见的头顶坍塌

二十七

你诞生在辞里时很软
像白木头
有皮肤的光泽

辞吧你变脆了
四面八方
摔碎你像满屋子面具

二十八

有人在这句话中说你
脚步声震动
这空荡荡的老房子

黑锈的风向标
油漆剥落
它等了很久才掐住你的喉咙

one piled up into another
the unknown faces are all the same face
while for a moment dissimilar words are all blank

26

you who are buried alive deep in a face
can just desperately curse
uninterrupted bad weather

corners of your eyes grown mouldy
headstone overgrown with moss
collapsing overhead where the dead can't reach

27

when you were born soft in words
like white wood
there was a sheen on your skin

words crisp you
from every quarter
smash you like a roomful of masks

28

there's someone talking about you in this sentence
the sound of footsteps shaking
this old deserted house

black-embroidered weathervane
paint peeling and falling
it has waited a long time to strangle you

二十九

面具从不对自己说话
寂静中一场谋杀
面具只流通面具间的语言

在死亡中咬文嚼字
神是一句梦呓
被满口牙秽剔出去

三十

你在海边的房子里看面具
当水光泛起
每张脸下无数张脸

一齐说话　粼粼
眼波把你淹没
你流走时认出万物是你

29

a mask never talks to itself
murder in silence
masks only circulate the language between masks

mincing words in death
gods are sleep talk
picked out by a mouthful of dirt between the teeth

30

you see masks in a room by the sea
as the water's gleam starts drifting
numberless faces below every face

talking together   crystalline shimmers
a liquid glance submerges you
as you flow away you recognise that all things are you

鳄鱼

一

鳄鱼用目光咬你
眼皮刀鞘般
藏起睡不着的牙齿

肉里条条小径
逼近水池
你被自己侧目一瞥咬死

二

嘴在别人脸上很庞大
你只剩一口假牙
残破墨绿的珊瑚

染着血　拉开腭骨
保持恫吓的姿势
屈服

三

死水中油腻腻的鳞片
你感到成群蚂蚁
正从骨缝间爬出

阵阵瘙痒地怀了孕
子宫像一座蚁冢
孵满天生食肉的鳄鱼

四

撕裂声有一种快感
骨骼尖叫的美
你的名字磨利你的牙齿

CROCODILE

1

the crocodile bites you with its vision
eyelids like scabbards
concealing unsleeping teeth

each little path in the flesh
that forcefully approaches the pond
you're fatally bitten by your own sidelong glance

2

the mouth in someone else's face is immense
all you're left is a mouthful of false teeth
dilapidated dark green coral

dyed in blood   pull the palate open
maintain a threat posture
surrender

3

greasy fish-scales in dead water
you feel ants swarming
climbing out from the sutures of your bones

pregnancy with a spasmodic troubling itch
womb like an anthill
brooding crocodiles born carnivorous

4

there's a delight in the sound of tearing
the beauty of the squealing skeleton
your name sharpens your teeth

你的血　与你分享
置他人于死地时
也再次杀死自己

五

谎言自泥泞骨髓中一击
你于重重甲胄下粉碎
断壁残垣

倒向周围
水藻在聆听
躯壳里空无一人的战争

六

凶杀之后饕餮之后
依旧会忏悔
像一连串饱嗝

或死者应有的歉意
为主胃里
消化不良的点点余腥

七

鳄鱼像一个字紧闭鼻孔
不屑理你
仅仅在这页白纸上浮沉

你绝望呼救
用潜伏已久的字
没入满是鳄鱼的水中

your blood   shares with you
when you put others in a deathtrap
and kill yourself again and again

5

as lying attacks from slushy bone marrow
you're shattered beneath your layers of armour
broken walls flattened and destroyed

fall in every direction
algae are carefully listening
a battle inside a deserted body

6

after murder after gluttony
you will repent as you always do
like a string of belches

or the apologies the dead must make
because left in god's stomach is
the tiny lingering rankness of indigestion

7

the crocodile's nostrils are sealed like a word
disdaining to notice you
merely floating on this white page

you despair of calling for help
with long-submerged words
sink into water full of crocodiles

八

茫然仇恨浸满一泓绿水
你的日子裹着
死者的皮肤度过

湿漉漉滑动
吊起　一张皮已足够
白夜似的炫耀乌有

九

许多世纪硬化的眼泪
丛生黑暗的老年斑
你温顺得无从被人挑剔

只盯住岸上的鱼
狠咬指甲
笨拙地掩饰起不停的饥饿

十

史前臃肿的爬行动物
把每天拖成影子
供一条街嚼食

咳嗽意味着灰尘
而唾液横流的早晨
又涂写出浑浊的笑容

十一

一个辞足以令你走投无路
只能隐入阳光
在无言中赤裸

8

vague hatred soaks the green waters
your crossing days wrap
the dead's skin

wetly sliding
lifting   a stretch of skin is enough
to show emptiness blazing like white night

9

tears hardened by many centuries
a growing cluster of dark liver spots
you're so docile there's no way you can be picked on

just stare at the fish on the bank
savagely biting your nails
stupidly concealing an endless hunger

10

bloated prehistoric reptiles
drag every day into the shade
supply a street to chew their food

coughing implies dust
but the morning overflowing with spittle
scribbles again those filthy smiles

11

one word is enough to close all exits
you can only hide in sunlight
naked in wordlessness

或埋没于幽暗躯体
皮肤下另一片月色
无须辞和衣服

十二

寂静不可逾越
鳄鱼白热的喘息更近
你骗自己时更耐心

都迷失于一枚松动的牙齿
漂浮的声音
你的沉默中到处是谎言

十三

你孤寂独坐的深夜里
太多鳄鱼静悄悄登陆
像不可触摸的诗

在五指间爬动
密集的草叶下
你不知不觉被咀嚼过多时

十四

每次构思预谋了你的存在
而第一个字捕杀你时
你被迫诞生

苍白的躯体越冷越庞大
你用一行诗推敲世界
于是真的死去

or be buried in the body of bleakness
another moonlight beneath your skin
needing neither words nor clothing

12

silence can't be surpassed
the crocodile's white hot panting is nearer
and when you cheat yourself, more patient

all lost in a loosened tooth
the floating sound
in your silence there are lies everywhere

13

in the night when you sit isolated and lonely
too many crocodiles come quietly ashore
like unreachable poems

creeping between five fingers
below the dense grass
you have long been unknowingly bitten

14

each time conception premeditates your existence
when the first word catches you and kills you
you are compelled to be born

the colder the pale body the more immense it is
you weigh up the world with a line of verse
and so have truly died

十五

你握着笔的手皮开肉绽
像被一条鳄鱼攫住
狂暴地扑向阳光

又无声溅落
笔被字攫住
鳄鱼腹中仍只有饥饿

十六

一个字长久地沉吟你
比窥测的鳄鱼
更静谧

咽喉又软又温暖
这黑暗甬道
看着你被节节删改出世界

十七

没有人掉进这行诗淹死
死者只是一个名字
和一具匿名的躯体

于是所有无人
挤满这行诗
偶尔浮出水面呼吸

十八

无人称的话里肯定有某人
或许是你
或另一个你

15

the skin on the hand that holds your pen has cracked and split
as if it had been seized by a crocodile
savagely pouncing on sunlight

and silently splashing down
pen seized by words
still only hunger in the belly of the crocodile

16

a word ponders you permanently
compared to a watching crocodile
more tranquil

the throat is soft and warm
this dark tunnel
watches you being deleted from the world bit by bit

17

no-one falls into this verse and drowns
a dead man is just a name
with a nameless body

so all the non-persons
crowded into this verse
sometimes float to the surface to breathe

18

there's definitely someone in non-personal speech
maybe it's you
or another you

于是所有无人
挤满这行诗
偶尔浮出水面呼吸

十九

用一个字忘掉年龄
在一行诗里任意衰老
年轻得侈谈死

就这么悬挂着
被钟声切开
静止于明亮的罪恶

二十

每个字注定是谎言
你仅仅依托着一页白纸
依托着葬礼上的银色花朵

其后　你也空白
与时间并肩流逝
象形地重申自己

二十一

你诅咒被日子抛弃
可这个字四堵高墙
时间也在孤零零逃亡

孤零零被你围困
你听到诅咒声
从四面八方的死寂中传来

but you're non-personal still
held by the crocodile's stubborn grip
you're terrified   you're all squeezed here

19

forget age with a word
grow old at will in a line
be young enough to waffle about death

hanging like this
sliced by the peal of bells
static in the clarity of crime

20

every word is doomed to be a lie
you utterly depend on the white page
the silver flowers of funerals

after   you are blank too
pass away shoulder to shoulder with time
pictographically reasserting yourself

21

you curse, abandoned by the days
but this word is within four high walls
time also escapes on its solitary way

solitary and under siege from you
you hear the sound of curses
carried by the deathly silence all around

二十二

一纸单薄的食谱囊括了岁月
于是你无时不在咀嚼
这饥饿的辞

浑身泥土
牙床的黄色化石
比你更近乎此刻

二十三

凝视一首诗
直到空白深处浮现五官
微笑精美如陷井

脸隐退　大眼眶的骷髅
盛满无字的晴空
终于读懂时已熨得很平

二十四

鳄鱼的寂寞五颜六色
被一滴水放大
雕铸成凶险的铜器

想象飞鸟陷入
天空的沼泽
有吞咽声蓝白相间

二十五

你在寂寞中搜索声音
鳄鱼或名字诱捕之后
死亡的哑剧

22

a flimsy recipe has bagged up the years
so you are continually chewing
this hungry word

mud everywhere
yellow fossilisation of the gums
nearer to this moment than you are

23

staring at a poem
till your senses emerge from the blank deeps
smile elegant as a snare

the face disappeared   big dry bones of eye-sockets
fill the clear analphabetic sky
once read and understood then ironed smooth

24

the crocodile's loneliness has all the colours it needs
magnified by a drop of water
cast and carved into a menacing vessel of bronze

imagine a flying bird falling
into the swamp of the sky
hearing the swallowing that alternates blue and white

25

in the silence you search for sound
after the trap of the crocodile or the name
the dumbshow of death

继续上演
谢幕的唯一动作
冗长的遗忘掌声雷动

二十六

这孩子满嘴鳄鱼的牙齿
慢慢长大　　膨胀
漂浮于空气中

似乎活着
一具死亡吐出的丑陋尸首
又被迟钝的生命舔食净尽

二十七

每个人背后跟踪一条鳄鱼
影子看影子是躯体
切齿声蜂拥而入

站成
饱食终日的一地影子
被厄运咬住沉沉甩动

二十八

在新的名字里你依旧缺席
从一个辞到另一个辞
你像隐身人一样行走

隐入一片蓝
风翻阅一个辞另一个辞
你不死　只是从未诞生

goes on with its show
the only action the curtain call
a redundant forgetting of thunderous applause

26

this child has a mouthful of sharp crocodile teeth
slowly growing   inflating
floating in the air

like being alive
an ugly corpse spat out by death
licked utterly clean by life again

27

behind everyone tracks a crocodile
a shadow sees a shadow as a body
swarm in to the sound of gnashing teeth

to stand and become
a field full of well-fed shadows
bitten by bad luck and thrown deep down

28

in your new name you're as absent as before
from one word to another word
you walk like an invisible man

hidden in a patch of blue
soar on the wind to read a word and another word
you don't die   it's just that you have never been born

二十九

话里有话　人里有人
岁月幻象丛生
磨擦你如鳄鱼肥厚的腹部

无数末日移入一个生日
呛死于一句活的谎言
你空白的影子不停走去

三十

死亡那不变的重量
落入鳄鱼的眼睛
你安详目睹自己被吞噬

伸手不见五指
才听清万物用冷血活着
一个字已写完世界

29

there is speech in speech   a person in a person
the hallucinations of the years grow wild
grinding you like the crocodile's fat belly

numberless dying days immigrate into one birthday
choked to death by the lie of living
your blank shadow endlessly walking on

30

death the unchanging weight
falls into the crocodile's eye
you serenely witness yourself being swallowed

only when it's so dark you can't see the five fingers of your
                                             outstretched hand
then you will clearly hear all creatures living with cold blood
one word has written a world

幸福鬼魂手记

给黄土南店，我插队三年的已消失的村子，
它继续看着我们变成自己的过去。

3. *from* Notes of a Blissful Ghost

To Yellow Earth Village—now vanished—
where I undrwent "re-education"
for three years during the Cultural Revolution:
it continues to watch as we become our own past.

幸福鬼魂手记

一.

漏出眼眶　狗拖着剥下一半的狗皮
跑　视野和一只被塞进火炉的麻雀比赛
飞

雪的触摸总腐烂了一半
断壁残垣遮住昨天
涂着　比白更少的颜色
地平线逆风弯回向一滴水冲刺

眼泪有只梨柄　牵着一大片叫嚷
幸福　幸福

二.

冬天是一个籍贯　明亮的猫
一跳　蹲在孩子脸上
爪子湛蓝就象地名
朵朵梅花悬空踩着一个冷的地名

拧紧孩子的肺
一棵古树向内拧着一下午现实
嘴里一大块玉
口音　什么都不说
就分泌母亲们的噩耗
弄脏阳光我们才复活

三.

进村的路醒在瓦砾下　土坯墙
楚楚可怜　象被张望的女孩

舌尖沁着一股咸味
冰就是她？继续背对窗外

NOTES OF A BLISSFUL GHOST

1

leaking from the eye-socket   dog dragging half-stripped dog skin
running   vision competes with stove-stuffed sparrow
flying

snow's touch always half-rotted
tumbledown ruins mask yesterday
painted   a colour less than white
horizon sprints back against the wind toward a drop of water

a teardrop has a pear-stalk   to lead a great hue and cry

bliss bliss

2

winter is home ground   bright shining cat
with one jump   squats on a child's face
claws sky-blue as a place-name
every plum flower hanging in mid-air, stepping on the place-name of
coldness

screws tight the child's lungs
an ancient tree twisted into an afternoon's reality
a large jade in the mouth
voice   says nothing
and secretes the worst of all news for mothers
we are only reborn when sunlight is soiled

3

the road to the village wakes under rubble   adobe wall
delicate and lovely   as a girl observed

tongue-tip tastes of salt
is the ice her?   her back still to the window

两手护住中心　能一吮而尽的鬼故事
裸着发育　风写的自传中

现在不停坍塌　西山的室内
一枚徘徊在零度的翡翠

把咸变香　缕缕逸出她没有的前世
鲜红的指头仍稔熟在冰下越界

越过　伤害杜撰的一千年
谁羞于作她臆想中的细节？

四.

世界不怕返回它熟知的过去
那儿乌鸦刨土　死者涮洗
一张旧照上必然的脸
昨夜栓在门口　蹭着棱角模糊的砖头
那只窜过草丛的狐狸
突然被床上一个嗓音喝住
白杨不怕返回　反着光耸出屋脊
那眼会变大的井蓄满不停的二十岁
仍不够发明一种没试过的吻
四只膝盖碰着　相爱的空壳间
繁星刚好迟到了一生
猫头鹰吃吃笑着人类的笑
出借月色　错过此刻就是幸福

五.

废墟否认谋杀

过去与时间无关

血不提问

失眠并非平行于天空

both hands shield the centre   a ghost story gone in one gulp
exposing growth   in wind-written confessions

the now endlessly collapses   an interior in the western hills
a piece of jasper hovering round zero

turn salt to fragrance   out blow wisps of the last life she never had
scarlet finger still familiar with crossing the boundary below the ice

crossing over   a millennium fabricated by hurting
who is too shy to be the detail of her fantasies?

4

the world is not afraid to go back to the past it knows so well
there crows scrape at the earth   the dead rinse out
a necessary face on an old photograph
last night tied in the doorway   rubbing worn brick
the fox just leaving a swathe of grass
suddenly called to a halt by a voice from the bed
aspens are not afraid to go back   to tower over rooftops reflecting light
the expandable well filled with twenty years of age that never stop
still not enough to invent an untried kiss
four knees colliding   inside the empty shell of love
the stars have just got here a lifetime late
the owl giggles at human laughter
loan out the moonlight   to miss this moment is bliss

5

ruins deny murder

the past has nothing to do with time

blood asks no questions

insomnia is not parallel to the sky

不存在公共地理学

活着无力活

光年从未溢出一个盲点

雪崩移开不了

完美的没有方向

六.

出租车浮起象艘火红的潜艇
拼贴在遗忘边缘
与一场土黄色风暴孤零零对峙

我们忘了　自己吓人的水深
一种谈论过去的口吻
仿佛从未驶过那片海域

七.

我已接受了任何一个地点
这个村子的角落　有雪
这场雪有小而晶莹的阳台
和塔　黄昏嗅嗅火车站
女儿在玻璃上贴满了星星
树妖在外面张贴夜　水
锁紧大门　目的地无限黑
迷人如妈妈用过的子宫

分娩穿着件羽绒衣的大鸟
拍打　空间毁于融雪声
弄湿一只耳朵　听到沉没

non-existent public geography

living with no strength to live

light years have never gushed from a blind spot

avalanches cannot move away

perfect non-direction

6

a taxi floats up like a fire-red submarine
collage in a forgotten margin
confronting alone a khaki storm

we have forgotten   the terrifying depth of waters inside us
a tone that speaks of the past
as if we had never crossed those seas

7

I have accepted any place
in a corner of this village   there is snow
the snow has small crystal balconies
and towers   twilight sniffs the station
a daughter studding the glass with stars
tree monsters posting up night outside   water
locking the door tight   destination infinite black
enchanting as the womb mother once used

that gives birth to a big bird in a down coat
flapping   space destroyed by the sound of melting snow
soaking an ear   hearing the sinking

八.

一条街倾斜滑向尽头一树梨花
过去　用力挤着水龙

喷　肉质的白尸骨的白

春天是一门外语
香的语法　精雕细琢
光　扇动每片花瓣背后浅黑的小漩涡

把推移的空　叫作现在
嫩嫩的手艺嵌着蓝
时间的首饰匠俯下身子　锉着
二月　银子打成的切削声如此悦耳
倒映人群洇开一滩墨迹

倒悬的瞳孔中街埋在自己地基下
迎向
喷来的　甜蜜的　泥泞

九.

两堵土坯墙归纳了全世界的时差

眼睛躲不开　尽管眺望是罪恶

断壁残垣慢悠悠坠落
自云中连成一片的墓地
梨花　自一个关于消失的思想

丢了的旧笔帽　和我们最美的性
辨认着幸福在这儿走出画框
被当作焦点　归纳全世界看不见的光

一幅死亡的静物中没有昨天
就象　没有今天

8

a street slides slanting down toward a pear tree in full blossom

the past   gives the fire hose a hard squeeze

spitting   the white of flesh and skeletons

spring is a foreign language
grammar of perfume   carved and polished with precision
light   stirring the little pale black eddies behind every petal

call elapsed emptiness   the now
immature craftsmanship inlaying the blue
time's jeweller bows down   filing
february   so sweet to the ear, the sound made by cutting metal
reflecting the crowd soaking the beach with ink marks

street hanging inverted in the eyeball
is buried under its own foundation
greeting
spat out   sweet   sludge

9

two adobe walls sum up time differences in all the world

eyes can't slip away   even though looking is a sin

tumbledown ruins unhurriedly decaying
from a cemetery made of clouds
plum blossom   from a thought about disappearing

the pen's old cap that was lost   and our beautiful sex
recognising that here happiness has walked out of the frame
taken as focus   summing up the light that all the world can't see

in the still life of death there is no yesterday
just like   there is no today

十.

不屑于赞同任何真实
幸福才珍藏谎言

十一.

　　没有无家可归的鬼魂。
　　没有归宿的是家：离脚下几步远，却被隔开。壕沟，纵横交错。
虚掩的枯草，夏天一定一人多高，现在遮着一口口陷阱。水泥块、钢
筋、旧电线，隐隐约约呲牙裂嘴。砖，左一堆右一堆，被烟熏黑过，
指出拆除的炕沿和灶台。残雪上一头小野兽留下爪印。风依旧在吹，
窗纸已不震抖、做响。报纸糊的顶棚一阵悉卒，那只老鼠黑亮的小眼
珠，朝下窥视着，从未料到会被人记住，就和房子、村庄、昨天一同
席卷而去。离脚下几步远，却到不了，那没人能证实曾存在过的世
界。
　　大片土坯墙、填平的池塘、一株柳树突然被认出的形状，发明了
一个人的象形文字。黄土，暴露就是遮掩，以暴露来遮掩。消失层层
堆起。家的幻象，比空地还空。我站在这里，比无人更少。呼吸的边
界，一排破栅栏，什么都挡不住，只显出过去那片活的废墟，如何泛
滥过来、撞上我、又推向身后。没有归宿的，是无尽落入眼眶的：一
片，实实在在，构成了，伤害的，虚无。
　　中秋节红肿的月亮，还插在亲吻的嘴唇之间，继续监听吗——当
《幸福鬼魂手记》，遍地呕吐出我们？

十二.

塔里也是河　漆黑地向上流动
天空　寒冷命运的库存
迫使两条鱼响应一个星座
看就被钓　一只银钩子钩进肉

象无用的美　躯体的河岸上
隐隐有路　有中国风景等在林子里

10
only when it disdains to endorse any truth
does happiness accumulate lies

11
there are no homeless ghosts.

home is what is homeless: a few steps away from where I stand, and I
will have been separated. ditches criss-crossed. unlatched dry grass, man-
high in summer, now concealing pitfalls. concrete blocks, reinforcing
bars, old electric cables, indistinctly bare teeth. bricks, heaps here and
there, smoke-blackened, revealing themselves as dismantled brick beds
and stoves. a small animal has left tracks on the slush. wind blowing
as always, paper window no longer trembling, no longer crackling.
newspaper-pasted ceiling rustles, the rat with its little black shining eyes
staring down, never expecting to be remembered by someone, is rolled
up and gone, along with the house, the village and yesterday. a few steps
away, and no-one can reach the world whose existence no one has ever
proved.

huge adobe walls, filled-in ponds, the suddenly-recognised shape of
a willow, has invented someone's pictography. yellow earth, to expose is
to cover up, covering up with exposure. disappearance piles up, layer on
layer. illusion of home, emptier than emptiness. I stand here, fewer than
nobody. frontier of breath, the line of a broken fence resisting nothing,
only showing how the living ruins of the past flood out to rush on me
and then push past me. What is homeless, is what endlessly falls into the
eye socket: a stretch of solidly-real, formed, destructive, nothingness.

inflamed red moon of mid-autumn festival, stuck between kissing
lips, will we still be watching when a blissful ghost's handbook vomits us
out everywhere?

12
in the tower is river too   flowing pitch-black upwards
sky   a stock of freezing fate
forcing two fish to answer a constellation
to look is to be hooked   a silver hook piercing flesh

like useless beauty   on the body's riverbank
is a faint path   and China's landscapes waiting in the woods

老桥丢下半个桥孔
跃入谎言　鱼自远方再引一点水

活就被约定　模拟建造一座塔的疯狂
秘密的漆黑湍急的力
甩着囚徒们　浑身鱼鳞地游在
锁住的起源

十三.

三是劫数

三年　借用一个人的形象溶解
她　远远走过水渠的那些她

粼粼变着　光逼近咒语
逼真的白影子填入行走中的轮廓
三个夏天的风重新油漆房间
多少吨绿报废时

水中那些器官空着
还来不及练习色情

就没了　血型的密码锁换了
三次　一支弦乐再也撕不下疼
到此为止　三数着无限
劫持这首诗　卅语满世界飞着找远去的耳朵

瞄准　下一个愚蠢的周期

十四.

被憎恨的地点　帮我想像
一条人生的虚线　星鱼贯而入
给窗口指定一个纬度
给老　准时上演熄灯后的黑暗
极光摇曳　屏风彩绘着美人
展翅　展览钉死的铁条

old bridge half its arch left
leaps into lies   fish pulling in yet more far-off water

to live is to be fated   simulating the madness of building the tower
secret pitch-black torrential force
flinging convicts   swimming all fish-scaled in
locked-up origin

13
three is the number of doom

three years   borrow someone's image to dissolve
her   those hers who far away walked over the ditch

shimmering and changing   light closes in on curses
lifelike white shadow fills in the walking silhouette
three summers' winds paint the room again
when so many tons of green are scrapped

in water those organs are empty
still not in time to practise lechery

and are no more   blood group's combination lock has been changed
three times   string music never again able to tear away pain
so far and no further   three counting infinity
kidnaps this poem   a whisper flying over the world in search of a far-off ear

take aim   at the next stupid cycle

14
detested place   help me imagine
a dotted line of life   stars come in one by one
assigning degrees of latitude to the window
for old age   punctually performing the darkness after the lamp is out
the aurora flickers   on the screen patterning beauties
spreading wings   exhibiting tightly nailed iron bars

恨而不得不停留之处
才咬住苦杏仁儿似的命运

十五.

嗅着
死者围巾里一股没带走的味儿
嗅　猛然记起活过的日子

味儿里的物质更滑腻而黑
这是你的空气
今晚　死者送来花朵

满屋浮动一双会搂抱的手
鼻子埋进坟墓编织的蕊
肺象另一只子宫在充血

温暖的刀口刻进你脖子
距离深呼吸　昏迷的致命的余香
让骗人的化学再欺骗一会儿吧

十六.

嗅着
过去中仅有的两个词　疼　或忘
死者逸出一条围巾时

世界比味儿更容易散去
梦象件银器　阴柔的黑玫瑰卷着边
却没味儿　你被留在梦之外

这个小小角落　被羊毛图案的膻腥
推着　嗅到了疼就还没忘
死者继续上楼　看表　吹笛子

边要你边筹备下一次死
味儿剜进骨缝　象一场猛烈苏醒的风湿
这是对谁都太陌生的现在

unable to leave the place I hate
till I have bitten the bitter almond of fate

15
smelling
in the scarves of the dead is a smell not taken away
smell   suddenly remember days that were lived

the material in the smell is greasier and blacker
this is your air
tonight   the dead present you with flowers

floating all through the room two hands that can embrace
nose buried in buds woven by the grave
lungs like another blood-congested womb

warm knife-edge carves into your throat
distance deeply breathing   the fatally lingering fragrance of coma
let cheating chemistry go on cheating for a while

16
smelling
the only two words in the past   pain   or forgetting
when the dead escape from a scarf

the world disperses more easily than a smell
dream like a piece of silverware   feminine black rose curling
but without smell   you are kept outside of dreams

this tiny corner   by the rank stink of patterned wool
pushed   if you smell pain you still haven't forgotten
the dead go on climbing the stairs   watching the clock   playing the flute

half wanting you half arranging the next dying
smell gouges into cracks in bone   like rheumatism violently coming to
this is a now too strange for anyone

十七.

水泥的音符堆满三月
从冬天望见的三月　鬼魂
别处预制的构件

运送千年才到了　燕子在村口索隐
零　狂暴扫描世界

断壁间某个元素在搅拌　灌注
善变的地貌温习一声口令
再变成集体的灰　春天剪齐心跳
立方的月色把合唱粘成一块

三月的挽歌中　燕子拖着磷光犹如凶器

田鼠无尽地掘一条隧道
询问一个封闭在石板下的季节
全家福被决定　乔迁到底片中

十八.

一首盲目以过去为主题的诗
茫然攀登一架水泥的梯子
她的脚趾甲倒竖半枚珍珠贝
他的踝骨　倒叙般鱼跃
拽着小腿的慢跑的旧胶片
性别放映林荫道上一场大火
她那两片刀刃温柔地磨快
他尝到切断玉米的甜
腰纠缠时云插进云
夜盈溢电波　沿脊椎呼啸而上
银白天线间雷霆一杯杯碰响
抚摸美妙坠毁　心跃入事故中途
二十岁的肖像越缩越小
耳垂玲珑　又含在嘴里玩
快感从发梢吐露尖尖的蛇信子
俯瞰　她一直领着狗吠
他的猫叼着自己天生的野

17

concrete's chords have filled up march
march seen from winter   ghost
components prefabricated elsewhere

arrive after a thousand-year shipping
swallows search for secrets at the village end
zero   violently scans the world

among broken walls some element is agitating   pouring
changeable landforms rehearse a password
turn to collective grey again   spring trims heartbeats
cubic moonlight glues the chorus together

in march's elegies   swallows drag lethal weapon-like phosphorescence

field mice endlessly digging a tunnel
inquiring about a season sealed in a flagstone
family photos decided   shifted to the negatives

18

poem which blindly takes what's passed as the theme
blankly climbing a concrete ladder
her toenail growing upwards a half oyster-shell
his anklebone   like a fish leaping in flashback
dragging the legs of an old slow-running film
sex projects a blaze on to the boulevard
she meekly sharpens her two-edged knife
he tastes the sweetness of cutting the corn
when the waist is tangled cloud penetrates cloud
night brimming with radio waves   whistles up the spine
between silvery aerials thunders the clink of glasses
caress a fabulous crashing   heart jumps in halfway through the incident
portrait at twenty smaller as it shrinks
earlobe exquisite   and nibbled for fun
ecstasy reveals pointed snake-tongues in tips of hair
overlooking   she has all along led a dog's barking
his cat holds its own innate wildness in its mouth

纵身跳下历史的墙头
一首诗没有主题
因为　没人过去

十九.

你的枕头紧挨一块麦田
你的梦　在空中拔节
闭着眼夜游的雪　一次迷路
迷失到水泥大厦的拼花地板上

篝火　自记忆洞口
漫天扬撒千万把亮晶晶的钥匙

野孩子的笑声扑入窗内
一根时间的细绳栓着你的耳鸣
荡回来　空间永远不会空
犹如口哨　隔着水泥墙
也把你惊醒了　月下磨利的镰刀
正割到你睡眠的根

二十.

被一场永无休止的内心谈话压垮
鬼魂就懂了
公园是能漫步的死后

婴儿们　借黑树枝迸发惨叫
鸟类迟钝地朝你投掷手雷

花象野鸽子落了一地
羽毛上撕下一团团紫色与白色
干梧桐果的性感悬在去年
老狗们喘息越来越慢
绿　躲在天边象恐怖分子
自言自语　操纵一场定时的大爆炸

没人能毁掉生活　除了你自己
毁了　就加入公园的冷　在春天

leaping down from the wall of history
a poem has no theme
because   no-one has passed by

19
your pillow is up against a cornfield
your dreams   burgeon in the sky
eyes closed sleepwalking snow   loses its way once
lost on the parquet floor of the concrete mansion

campfire   from memory's cave mouth
scatters the sky with ten million glittering keys

wild child's laughter swoops in the window
twine of time tying up your tinnitus
swinging back   empty space is never empty
just as a whistle   beyond a concrete wall
wakes you with a start too   in moonlight a sharpened sickle
is scything the roots of your sleep

20
crushed by the unending internal dialogue
ghosts understood
the park is where the dead can post-mortem wander

babies   use black boughs to burst out wailing
birds slowly hurl grenades toward you

flowers falling all around like wild pigeons
purples and whites all torn off their feathers
dried parasol-tree fruit hangs sexily in last year
old dogs pant slower and slower
green   hides at the horizon like a terrorist
talking to himself   controlling a huge timed detonation

no-one can destroy life   unless you yourself
destroyed   and joined the cold of the park   at springtime

二十一.

以为过去时中有一个过去　正如
疯子坚信眼中有一个世界
牛群隔着雪亮的水晶体
看我们的球形　草场　战争　邻居
刚散开的一夜　抽空水洼的湿
以为屠宰能还原成一种风格

以为剥剩一张牛皮的还是牛
靴子捻着金黄而软的本质
我们穿上　坚信又一次发明了血
动词一变就响起流淌声
流入　舌尖后面转着虚无的水晶骰子
疯狂始于用替身说话的一刹那

二十二.

废墟里的幸福　来自老
丢在身后黑暗中的断齿
听见风更猖獗的联想
白昼越拆散　夜越给你机会
装订富有的谎言

二十三.

肉体延伸村子最偏僻的一角
春天焚毁　溃烂　坍塌　就是装修一新

末日象一堂地理课
每个人打开的风景　只有自己能看见

雪纪念性地飘　乱石静静孵着
导游图　叶子睁大盲眼查找

鬼魂现实中一排花簇沿街点燃鞭炮
活人记得　玉兰朝天高擎酒杯

21

thinking there is a past in past tense   just like
a madman is convinced there is a world in the eye
herds of cows through the snow-bright crystal lens
watch our sphere   grasslands   war   neighbours
a night just dispersed   pumps wetness from puddles
thinking butchery can still be restored as a style

thinking a stripped cow skin is still a cow
boots grinding the essence golden and soft
we put them on   convinced we've invented blood once again
verbs change and the sound of flowing begins
flowing into   the crystal dice behind the tongue spinning nothingness
madness begins from the instant we use substitutes to speak

22

bliss in the ruins   comes from old age
broken teeth left in the dark behind you
hearing the wind free-associating more rampantly still
the more day is dismantled   the more night gives you the chance
to bind a richer lie

23

flesh extends to the remotest corner of the village
spring incinerated   ulcerated   caved-in   is fixed up all new

doomsday like a geography lesson
the landscape everyone opens   only yourself can see

snow drifts commemoratively   rubble quietly incubating
a tourist map   leaves open blind eyes wide to search

in ghost reality rows of bouquets light firecrackers along the street
the living remember   magnolias raising their goblets toward the sky

皮肤自古沿用的盛血的塑料袋
磨破　翻飞　挂满灌木

嚓嚓剪刀声　不吝惜脚步声
细心剥吧　一滴眼泪中总不乏死鸟的出处

二十四.

手记删去了手　死者的名字
给红色电话簿丢下密码
窗外　勤奋的地平线一直在破译
　　　臆想的终点也太奢侈
水就是房间　诗人明亮变形的波浪
不流　忍受着一行诗比白更少的颜色
　　　换一只桌上的骨灰瓮也太奢侈
光　在天上每月精雕细刻
血自女孩狐狸腰身内
激射而出　花朵都象女巫
鬼魂定居在地名里无视世界来来去去
每个人的地图上自己是雨季
　　　墙太奢侈　腐蚀的知识
令浴缸里一付骸骨永远酷热
音节的梳子　梳过草坪金黄的阴毛
表盘上三百六十度的废墟
肯定　死亡没有不同的语言
　　　诗人哪儿也返回不了
野蛮古老的美是我们唯一知道的美
时代被用尽　而一行诗的血腥还远远不够
加深一场过不去的风暴
　　　重申此夜　鬼魂幸福的初夜

skin the plastic bag used for all time to hold blood
wears out   dances in air   drapes the bushes

snick-snack of scissors   ungrudged footsteps
peel with great care
a teardrop is never short of dead birds' origins

24
the handbook has deleted the hand   names of the dead
leave behind a code for the red phone book
outside the window   the hardworking horizon has been decoding all
along
to conjecture an ending is too extravagant
water is a room   the poet's shining metamorphosed waves
don't flow   enduring a colour less than the white of a line of poetry
to change an urn on the table is too extravagant
light   carves and polishes with precision in the sky each month
blood from inside a girl's foxy waist
shoots out   flowers are all like witches
the ghost settles down in place names oblivious to the world coming and
going
on everyone's map everyone is the rainy season
wall is too extravagant   knowledge that corrodes
makes the bones in the bath eternally swelter
comb of syllables   has combed across the golden pubic hair of the lawn
three hundred and sixty degrees of ruin on the dial
affirm   death has no different language
the poet has nowhere to return
wild old beauty is the only beauty we know
time is spent   but the smell of blood in a line of poetry is far from
enough
deepening a storm that cannot pass
reiterate this night   ghost's first night of bliss

十六行诗

4. Sixteeners

伦敦

现实是我性格的一部分
春天又接受了死者四溢的绿
街道　接受更多鲜花下更黑的送葬队伍
雨中红色的电话亭犹如一个警告
时间是内脏的一部分　鸟类的口音
打开长椅上每张生锈的脸
看着夜色的眼睛一场冗长的飞行事故
又一天被涂掉时　伦敦

写尽我的疯狂　舔尽啤酒的棕色泡沫
钟声在一只鸟头里震荡象阴暗失业的诗句
城市是辞的一部分　我最可怕的部分
显示我的渺小　接受
窗外霉烂的蓝色羊皮封面
羊肉们的记忆勤奋装订着
自己的死亡　死在　不抽搐的镜头里
当两页报纸间是墓地　墓地后边是大海

水的归程

这还是溢出一只六岁时小小浴缸的血
这还是那张票　在手里攥了多年
攥紧一艘死亡的渡轮
岸　明确得象一道肉体的界限
疼　就比铸铁栏杆更准时
切开湖水的光摔碎在眼睛后面
雪山的大教堂　摔进堆不满的蓝
盯着天空中被漂白的脸逼近

长长的尾线悬挂你一生的地图
一只死鸽子的翅膀垂下
水把过去收藏得更深　回顾
双手再也无从错过不在的
你的血还乘着一个肉色坍塌的地点
还忍受着湖上最后的周末
虽然一只破纸袋已抖空了多年
喂鸽子的老妇人　本身已彻底是残骸

LONDON

reality is part of my nature
spring has accepted the overflowing green of the dead again
streets   accept more funerals which are blacker yet beneath the flowers
red phone boxes in the rain like a warning
time is part of the internal organs   bird voices
open every rusting face on the benches
watching night's eyes a prolonged flying accident
when yet another day is blotted out   London

write out all my madness   lick out all the brown beer's froth
the bell's toll in a little bird's brain vibrates like a gloomy verse unemployed
the city is part of the word   the most terrifying part of me
showing my insignificance   accepting
blue mildewed sheepskin slip-cover outside the window
sheep meat's memory diligently binding
its own death   dying in   the non-convulsing lens
when between two pages of newsprint is a grave   behind the grave is the
ocean

WATER'S RETURN JOURNEY

this is still blood overflowing from little bathtub at six years old
this is still that ticket   gripped many years in the hand
tightly gripping the ferryboat of death
shore   explicit as the limits of flesh
pain   more punctual than cast-iron railings
light that cuts lake water open shatters behind the eyes
snowy mountain cathedral   tumbles into unpileable blue
bleached face staring at the sky presses in close

on the rope's long end hangs the map of all your life
a dead pigeon's wings drooping
water stores the past even deeper   look back
and both hands have no way again to let what's not there slip away
your blood still riding the crumbling flesh-coloured site has nowhere to turn
still enduring the final weekend on the lake
though a crumpled paper bag has been shaken empty for years
the old woman feeding the pigeons   is herself another wreck

塔中的一夜

黑暗才是我们寻找的　而窗户
无一不是眩目的凶猛动物
看过的雪隔开从眼睛到眼睛的距离
鸟　布置苍白裸体上的磷光
石头旋转成反锁自己的角落
让我们的肉互相被反锁
夜才是必须的　一块皮肤的
一夜　聆听四面悬崖下总不够寂静的风暴

天空总不够不存在的深度
手指移动在睡眠上　日晷生锈的针
没有时间　才有女性触摸自己的疯狂
塔比我们的嗅觉更享受囚徒脆弱的咸味
痛苦　更爱好一切无法治逾的
被黑暗暴露在某处　我们
一再找到彼此深处　喝醉
成为不愿醒来的　一再　推迟这黎明

布痕瓦尔德的落日与冷

末班车还没来　而暮色的时刻表
已四合　最后的光移出水银柱
最初的冷正脱下淡红色皮肤
等车的我们　等着落日
把一天变成一间熄了灯的图书阅览室
夜来自一次肉体的内分泌
黑暗的领座员领着石头
枝头静下来精雕细刻的乌鸦珍珠

山下就是生活　去那儿只要轻轻一跳
如落日　在铸铁围墙后无尽落下
冻疼的指尖上一粒百年钟声的水晶
一小堆用骨头收藏的灰
抚摸就在查阅　伤害的薄薄词典
消失到零下的地平线　裸露
水泥阴道里一滴硬得象行星的精液
等在无人的未来　末班车早过了

A Night in the Tower

darkness is what we look for   and windows
none is not a savage beast dazzling
snow that has been seen separates the distance from eye to eye
bird   fixes phosphorescence on pale naked bodies
stone gyrates to become the corner that locks itself in
letting our flesh be locked out from each other
it's night that is needed   a piece of skin's
single night   listening to the never quiet enough storms below the cliffs

the sky is never deep enough for non-existence
finger moving on sleep   gnomon of a rusty sundial
only when there's no time   is there the madness of a woman touching
                                                        herself
the tower enjoys the salt reek of prisoners' weakness more than our noses do
pain   loves all that is incurable
exposed somewhere by the dark   we
search for each other's depths over and over   drunk
become unwilling to wake   again   postpone this dawning

Sunset and Cold at Buchenwald

the last train isn't here yet   but the twilight timetable
is closing in   the final light has gone out from the mercury column
the first cold just taking off pink skin
we who wait for the train   are waiting for sunset
to turn the day into a reading room after lights out
night comes from a secretion of the flesh
the attendant of darkness is leading stones to their seats
branches calm down intricately-carved raven pearls

down the hill is life   you need only tread lightly to go there
like the setting sun   endlessly sets behind the iron parapet
on a frostbitten fingertip the tiny crystal of a century's bell
a small heap of ash collected by bones
to stroke is to consult   the slim dictionary of hurt
the horizon vanished below zero   exposing
in the cement vagina a drop of semen hard as a planet
waiting in an unpeopled future   the last train long gone by

可能的室内乐

神经的雷达在天上搜索
重逢却是一个休止符　重新
夹起十八岁　你和我原来象两根手指
夹紧象生日的一天
要疼痛就双倍疼痛　要远
一房间雨声就脱掉血那边的衣服
丢了的碧玉耳环挡着骨头
纸叠成形而上　每封信写在五月

象返回噫语的一只铃
十八年前的诗发育成另一个女孩子
是你的　粉红子宫里小小签名是我的
以世界为半径　春夜
摸遍一只羊羔甜香的体内
要作你眼中那个字就得比字
更黑　一滴金黄琥珀的泪
捧着　空　甚至别碰坏这难忍的距离

海的慢板

痛苦必须有它自己的角落　例如午夜
例如窗口　大海的粘膜贴着玻璃
黑暗的物质从眼睛里缓缓渗出
红酒象一盏夜航灯
你听见浑身血脉的入海口叫喊一个名字
变冷的告别翻开了课本
远方一块黑板　悬在零点的赤裸之外
波浪背诵一张脸的家庭作业

反光的诗　反射鱼类诞生前的思想
一千条水平线推迟大海这个词
岛屿屈从的肉　冲撞不能推迟的今天
正如每天　眺望就是隔开
四周吱吱喳喳的玻璃被你吸进肺里
比不动还慢的死角　坐进
醉意　风暴过滤成另一侧无色的现实
痛苦　它完美无缺　它是瞎子

CHAMBER MUSIC OF POSSIBILITY

the radar of nerves is searching the sky
but reunion is only a silent beat   again
squeezing eighteen years of life   you and I just like fingers
tightly gripping a single day of like a birthday
if there's pain it's doubled   if there's distance
the sound of rain in the room undresses beyond the blood
a lost jade earring is blocking bones
papers pile up metaphysics   every letter written in May

like a bell going back to ravings
poems from eighteen years ago growing into another girl
are yours   the tiny signature in a pink womb mine
with the world as its radius   the spring night
caresses the sweet-smelling inside of a lamb's body
whoever wants to become the word in your sight must be blacker
than that character   one golden amber teardrop
held   empty   so don't even break this unbearable distance

LENTO FOR THE SEA

pain must have its own corner   midnight for instance
a window for instance   ocean's mucous membrane pasted to the glass
the substance of darkness slowly leaks out from the eye
red wine like a navigation light
you hear the estuary of every vein in your body cry out a name
a farewell turned cold has opened the textbook
a distant blackboard   hangs outside the nakedness of zero
waves endlessly memorising the homework of a face

a poem reflecting light   reproduces pre-natal thoughts of fish
a thousand horizons postponing the word 'ocean'
flesh that islands submit to   collides with the today that cannot be postponed
exactly like every day   to look from afar is to partition
the glass chattering all around is breathed into your lungs
a dead space slower than immobility   sits into
drunkenness   storm filtered into another colourless reality
pain   it's perfection   it's a blind man

口　琴

鲜花在寒冷的天空下显得怪诞
只有嘴唇是例外　河水
用一首歌雕琢小小的耳朵
往事的舌尖细细舔进一块空地
半音半音的石头在靠岸还是离岸
春天吸着还是吐着　光的还是鱼骨的簧片
谁在风中抖动一个人的旧地图
把辞变没就不算谎言

世界象云　一吹就响
嫩绿的手指学习耳语时
疼痛找到你　比未来更长久
生活简单得只象这次生活
河水流去　还是用一枚泛白的指甲
在此刻越掐越深　演奏
还是给古老银亮的　没有皮肤的再按上指纹
再爱一次音箱里漆黑的来历

明　代

没有谁死于现在　桥那边就是过去
美人水袖中三百年美学
梦见鸟梦游瓦　船
撑到床前　身上的小溪流淌一夜
木头窗棂里一件月光的袍子
换下　死亡近似一个被解决的难题
动词雪白的手心瞧着
不动　桥那边在我们这边

每个街角上孤零零悬挂着皇帝
路灯　照见时间楚入钟表
一个肉体的精密结构拧紧了弦
体温里定居的愚蠢朝代
我们挥霍的美不在乎被一阵寒战推翻
醒　涮洗深及呼吸的雕花陷阱
桥那边　明代在暗处
记得这样活　鬼魂派出现在的知识

Harmonica

under a cold sky the flowers have an absurd look
only their lips exceptional   the river's waters
carve small ears with a song
tongues of the past delicately lick into vacant ground
semitone by semitone stones moor and don't unmoor
springtime inhales and still vomits   what's bright is still the fish bone reeds
who shakes someone's old maps in the wind?
making words sink doesn't count as a lie

the world is like clouds   blow and it sounds
when tender green fingers learn to whisper
pain will find you   for longer than the future
life will be simplified to being just like this life
the river's waters flow away   still with a whitening fingernail
right now the more pinched the deeper   still performing
for the ancient silver   skinless pressing the fingerprints again
loving one more time the jet black source in the speakers

The Bright Ming Dynasty

nobody dies in the now   over the bridge there is the past
in a beauty's long sleeves three centuries of aesthetics
dream a bird's dream of travelling the tiles   boat
poled to the bedside   the body's brook running all night
a gown of moonlight in the wooden window frame
discarding   a death quite similar to a problem solved
 the verb's snow-white palm watching
unmoving   here by us is over the bridge there

on every street corner hangs a solitary emperor
streetlights   illuminate time loitering in clocks
with the flesh's precise structure time twisted the string tight
a stupid dynasty settled in body temperature
the beauty we squander doesn't care about being cancelled by a shiver
waking   rinses a carved trap deep as breathing
over the bridge there   the bright Ming in the dark
remember to live like this   ghosts send out knowledge of the now

171

菩 提

松鼠的四肢里遍布现实的内伤
那仰天抽搐的姿势
毋宁是色情的
谁全力以赴投入这个清脆的秋天
一枝插进血管的体温计　插在窗口
让叶子们象攀援的豹
匆匆跳下梦失踪的另一半
谁猛然自你体内抽出　丢下虚无

语言在水上消失　风把字带走
又一个故事只有读者却没有作者
这绿色眼神　来到就是痛苦
每年一只最后摘除的乳房
摇着　听着一夜象婴儿无情地咂嘴远去
一个人被再次解散为时间
坐在　一棵词义碧蓝的树下
象坚持冷　坚持去错

形 式

你的黑暗挑选医院的颜色
体内的风声　刮到体外就成了金属的
针尖划过　真空的疼
再制作一只人形的笼子
鲜鱼的血肉擦洗四面钉入的钉子
海鸥骑上整早晨的光
眼中的速度一场雪白的手术
默许一个前世再发生一次

不纯　你女孩似的胸脯躲不开
坠落的翅膀两只血淋淋的粉扑
太纯　大海药香的齿轮间
鸟类的圆眼睛什么也不看
那缝满了羽毛的蓝　被找到时如此真
正象你要的　谎言
醒来　梦漏掉象双手试图捧住的水
再次依赖人脆弱的缝隙

Linden Tree

squirrel limbs are spread all over the internal injuries of reality
convulsing face-up in that position
rather say it's sexual
someone throws themselves into this melodic autumn with all their strength
a thermometer stuck into the vein   stuck in the window
lets leaves resemble climbing panthers
rushing to jump down the half-vanished dream
someone abruptly pulls from your body   lost nothingness

language disappears on the water   the wind bears the words away
another story has only a writer and no reader
the green light in the eyes   comes with pain
every year the final excised breast
rocking   listening all night to a baby-like merciless sucking fading away
a person repeatedly disintegrated into time
sitting under   a tree whose meaning is as azure the word
like persisting with cold   persisting with going wrong

Form

your darkness picks out the colours of a hospital
wind in the body   blew outward and has become metal
needle point has scratched   the pain of the vacuum
to make another human-shaped basket
fish flesh has scrubbed the nails hammered in all around
seagulls riding the light of the entire morning
snow-white surgery speed in the eye
acquiescence in a previous life appears again

impure   your girlish breast cannot escape
dropping bloody wings two powder puffs
too pure   between the gears of the medicinal-smelling ocean
the round eyes of birds see not a thing
find   that feather-stitched blue real as this
just like the lie   you want
waking   dreams ebb away through the fingers like water
again and again relying on the cracks in human fragility

地中海

没有一个昨天不起源于现在
就象　没有一个现在能够被聆听
恐怖的蓝夷平了美人和图书馆
大火继续焚烧在耳膜上
大理石堆砌耳鼓深处的白色污垢
一只水鸟的短促汽笛声
漆满阳光的峭崖日日沉没
腐烂的海床上　我们没什么可迷失

游泳池下临山谷
我们保持跃出的一刹那
孤悬空中的躯体犹如神话
尴尬地渴望与水之赤裸肌肤相亲
模拟水　永远不在
无关听力地溢满这只石刻的耳廓
听到天空　脱下湿淋淋的丝织戏装
死一次就够了

光
　　　　　————"流神聚水"（道符）

坐在庭院里　看一只柠檬聚集大海
坐进枝头金黄的那一滴
看　自己瞳孔中湛蓝漆黑的
距离在窗台上慢慢回头
鸟鸣的小巧机器在松针间
最远的栏杆一双翩翩鸟翅
重复画下那椭圆　嵌着三片云
坐进柠檬的光速

蕊是一场爆炸
庭院象一只核碎到空中
光在聚集眺望的静脉
鲜艳的肉体打开一扇屏风
一只柠檬里死亡的亮度灼瞎了
金黄的围困视线里的疼
看　鸟儿心跳的高度
自己瞳孔中　唯一不可见的瀑布

174

MEDITERRANEAN

there's no yesterday that hasn't risen from now
just like   there's no now that can be heard
terrifying blue smoothes out beautiful women and libraries
fire rages on across the membranes of the ear
marble clutters the white filth of the eardrum's depth
a waterfowl's brief siren skins the ear
steep cliffs of painted sunlight sinking down daily
on the rotten bed of the sea bottom   we have nothing to lose

below the balcony overlooking the valley
swimming pool retains the instant of leaping
our lonely bodies hang in mid-air like legends
awkwardly yearning to kiss the water's naked skin
simulating water   always absent
indifferent to hearing overflowing an ear carved of stone
hearing the sky   take off its sopping wet silken costume
dying once is enough

LIGHT
floating divinities gather the waters (Taoist charm)

sit in the courtyard   watch a lemon gather the sea
sit into the golden-branched drop
watch   what's blue-black in the pupils of your eyes
distance on the window-sill slowly looking back
little exquisite chirping machines of singing birds in the pine needles
furthest railings a pair of graceful dancing wings
repeatedly painting that oval   inlaid with three clouds
sit into the lemon's speed of light

stamens are an explosion
courtyard like a kernel spat into the sky
light is gathering the veins that are looking far away
colourful flesh opens a screen door
light   long ago blinded by death's brightness in the lemon
to be gold is to surround the pain in your field of vision
watch   the height of the bird's heartbeat
in the pupils of your eyes   the only invisible waterfall

龙华寺

被鳄鱼咀嚼构成这首诗的前夜
梦中可怕的真　寺
院　在水滨在山巅
只要手的莲花仍象那天一瓣瓣掰着
空　我们的抵达半是梅半是血
只要许愿的冷能停留
在香炉里　照像机片段片段的活
青苔捻了又捻石头的眼珠

找到这首诗的前世
骸骨搂着骸骨　漫步于钟声的背面
我们的猜测定居在一朵蓓蕾里面
梅飘落搅拌好香的血
膝下泄露的血迹　重新从一数到七
只有信回来的　回味着
闪光灯　潜望刚刚成形的肉体
依稀记得与鳄鱼性交的快感既美又疼

河口上的房间

总有一只船远去　目送着你
对岸在远去　天空是倒立的命题
字与字之间一条河流过
到你的无言时　海鸥的旗语雪白而膻腥
退潮　月亮在拉溺死者的名字
鱼类俯瞰黄昏　眼眶中抠出灯塔
每天的镜子关紧一个葡萄酒味儿的
上游　黑暗象一盘海鲜逆流行驶

大海从一个问句开始　它问　哪儿
房间象一只鸟站在船桅上
四壁漂流的地址　演奏桥的弦乐
手指与手指之间只有水不动
远去的是你　总比一个远方更远
目送一首诗　浸入总在渐冷渐蓝的体温
雾来了　雾是夜的闸
你知道合上眼这清晨就在海里

Longhua Temple

being chewed by the crocodile structured the eve of this poem
in dreams the terrifyingly real   temple court-
yard   at the water's edge on the mountain peak
only if the hand's lotus still opens like that day petal by petal
emptiness   our arrival half plum half blood
needs only the cold of a vow to stay
in the incense burner   the fragmentary life of a camera
twisted moss twists the stone's eyeball again

the eve of finding this poem
skeleton hugging skeleton   strolls behind the silence of the bells
the direction of our surmise settled in a bud
plums drift down to blend with perfumed blood
bloodstains leak out from behind the knee   from numbers one to seven again
only to believe what comes back   enjoying in memory
flashbulbs   periscoping the newly-formed flesh
we vaguely remember the pleasure of sex with crocodiles was lovely and sore

Room by the Estuary

there's always a boat going far away   watching you go
the other shore is going far away   the sky an inverted thesis
a river flows by between word and word
until when you are speechless   seagull semaphore is snow-white and rancid
ebb-tide   the moon is pulling the names of the drowned
fish overlook twilight   lighthouses fished from eye sockets
the mirror of every day fastens a wine-flavoured
upstream   darkness like a plate of seafood rushes against the tide

the ocean begins with a query   it asks   where
the room stands like a bird on the mast
an address of four drifting walls   playing the bridge's string music
only water unmoving between finger and finger
what's going far away is you   always further than far away
gazing after a poem   immersed in a body temperature colder and bluer
mists come   mists are night's floodgate
you know with eyes closed that dawn is in the ocean

十年

时间象一尾鱼游向自己的美味
岸不在你脚下　年
比一个字更空　防波堤
尖尖的乳头喂着风暴
石头不在　你象一颗铜螺丝被拧着生锈
波浪闪光的腋窝里　沉船纪念碑
以一个穿戴鱼鳞的名字
冲下肉的坡度　蜇着海蜇的艺术

这片空白被称为水　变甜
被称为老　阳光有一块磁铁内在的紧
十个夏天在你肺里
修剪　一处失血花园的黑色水位
港口的倒影跳着舞
努力回忆　谁留下酷似你的性
厨房里一杯自酿的酸啤酒被喝掉
等于被倒掉　骸骨毕业于又一个零

双城记

茫然比花岗石还硬　梨花
延长电话里一片盲音
耳鸣似的白　悬挂另一个春天的卧室
脚步拆卸成零件　装配鲜艳的地址
旱冰场储存着死了的香味儿
你的同名人　一具远走高飞的裸体
被街道搭在云端的铝制梯子开除
欲望提醒　另一场雨下了整夜

春天剥掉肥沃的衬裤
梨树原地不动　攀登进电话簿
的抽象　阳台一团阴暗
时差在一寸深的往事里抽丝
天空分开鲜红湿润的两小片
吮着你头骨中的复数
双倍虚拟一个存在　玷污你的不在
梨花冷冷组织起玻璃面具和沼泽

Ten Years

time swims fish-like towards its own fine flavour
the shore is not beneath your feet   years
emptier than a word   breakwaters'
sharp nipples feeding the storms
the stones are not there   you corrode like a twisted brass screw
in the armpit of the waves' light   shipwreck monument
with a name that wears fish-scales
dashing down the slope of flesh   stinging jellyfish art

this blank is called water   sweetened
it's called old   sunlight has the inner tightness of a magnet
ten summers in your lungs
trim   black water-level of a garden of blood loss
the harbour's inverted image is dancing
assiduously remembering   who has left behind a gender like yours
in the kitchen a fermenting glass of sour beer is drunk off
same as being poured away   the graduate skeleton spits out another zero

A Tale of Two Cities

vacancy is harder than granite   pear blossom
extends the blind sounds from the phone
white like tinnitus   hangs in the bedroom of another spring
stripped-down footsteps   assemble a gaudy address
the roller rink accumulating the dead perfume
your namesake   a naked body flying high and far away
expelled by the street's aluminium ladder hanging on the clouds
desire reminds   another rain shower it's been falling all night

spring strips away its fertile underwear
pear tree not moving from its place   climb into the phone book's
abstraction   balconies a mass of gloom
time difference is reeled off the cocoons of the inch-deep past
the sky separates into two moist scarlet pieces
sucking on the plurals of your cranium
doubly supposing a single existence   sullying your absence
pear blossom coldly organises the glass masks and the swamp

回忆录

回忆录完成于一次生活之前
键盘上的雨声发明衰老
珠宝出土　我在一个形象里
远眺跳远的袋鼠
追赶一块精液四溢的黄昏的玉
候鸟雪白　吐出了地平线
一页肉质乐谱的因袭美学
把一根油腻腻的绳子拉过

身上最怕疼的河道
回忆录回忆着删节的速度
说"是"　教唆一头小狼牙齿伶俐
雨学会情人软软的咬
花岗石象一大块海绵吸净每分钟
又是嫩嫩的终点
又有歪曲的天才　让死鱼银光闪闪
追上　活人永不敢追上的一首诗

柏林．STORKWINKEL　12号

死亡的戏剧扭歪了你们的五官　已没人
记得一阵孱弱儿童的笑声和恐惧
门廊空空荡荡　树是一柱香
九月押送着全世界的金币
用世俗的怪僻擦亮这个黄铜号码
楼梯的脚本　夸张房间里一顶帽子
一个不出众的时代高高站直
捏碎大海的风筝　血　从没有童话

只有　死者被恢复的善仍走在回家的路上
落叶干枯的刃平静地割下秋天
一封信不出众的谎言　你们的名字
偷换成我们的　鬼魂是一张旧照片
杰作太熟知怎样烹调人的缺陷
润色孩子们掌心里一幅星图
谁躲进风声了　别再掉进脚丫的黑牡蛎
死吧　诗是唯一的地址值得去复活

MEMOIR

a memoir is completed before a one-off life
the sound of rain on the keyboard invents old age
jewellery excavated   in one image I
watch kangaroos bouncing into the distance
pursuing the twilight jade that overflowing semen
migrant buds' snow-white   has sicked up the horizon
the carried-over aesthetics of a page of the fleshy score
has tugged on a greasy rope

through river channel that most fears pain in the body
memoir recalling the speed of abridgement
says 'yes'   inciting the little wolf to make its teeth smart
rain learns the soft soft bites of lovers
granite like a great sponge sucks each minute clean
it's the tender terminus again
there's talent perverted again   making the silver shine of dead fish
catch   a poem the living have never dared to catch

12 STORKWINKEL, BERLIN

death's drama has skewed your senses   nobody
remembers the laughter and terror of a scatter of frail children
the porch utterly empty   tree an incense stick
September escorting all the gold in the world
polishing up the brass number with worldly eccentricity
the staircase script   exaggerates a hat in the room
an unexceptional era stands straight and tall
crumbling the ocean's kites   blood   has never had a fairytale

only   restored virtue of the dead still walks the homeward road
withered blades of fallen leaves silently mow the autumn
a letter unexceptional lying   your names
switched with ours   ghost an old photograph
masterpieces know too well how human flaws are cooked
polishing up a star chart in children's palms
who has ducked into the wind's sound   don't drop into the foot's black
                                                                    oyster
die   poetry is the only address worth being reborn in

十六行

辞　越来越深地吸进一个人
疯狂教你与你的血缘和解
十六颗莲子　一一剜出眼珠
被一行泪提在手上时苦涩
鸟儿的水晶针管抽满蓝色时清香
十六座园林　女儿们靠在鱼背上
咳出了肺　一点红是一幅天象图
疯狂教你最疯的景致还远远关在窗内

象期待毁灭的年龄
呕出一个日子　铺满你的桌子
旧照在变薄　十六张脸谱描慕一种消失
等到这形式　发育你另一半血肉
十六个朝代玩着倒影　寻觅
一次受限于死者酷热的机会
你听见　某只回声四起的空空的胃
呕着传统

一只苏黎世的天鹅

如他所说　幸福有一种挽歌的形式
挽留它自己不知道的美
舞蹈的流水　假寐了七百年
向石拱桥上那人匆匆一瞥
如她所说　挽回不了就一口口去咀嚼
扑入腋下的又一场白雪
橙红色小嘴依次伸向似曾相识的岸
肉体的热忱　热衷于放弃

抽搐的羽毛笔　签署过再多垂死
仍是单数　如他站在水面上说
如她　认出倒影中冷冷重叠的唯一一只
在河底甩着断翅　说　阳光嚼烂了
五指之美美在死死握紧茫然
泄露内心的蓝　衬得一根银制链条更刺眼
弯成它自己血污的首饰
肯定一只大鸟的狂暴　挽歌般安详

SIXTEENER

a word   inhales a person deeper and deeper
madness reconciles you to your blood kin
sixteen lotus seeds   gouging out eyeballs one by one
harshened when carried in the hand of a line of tears
fragrant when the bird's crystal needle is drawn full of blue
sixteen gardens   daughters leaning on fishes' backs
coughing out their lungs   a drop of red is a star map
madness teaches you the maddest view still shut far away inside the window

like the age waits for destruction
spat out a day   all over your table
old photos are thinner   sixteen painted masks admire a disappearance
wait for this shape   to grow the other half of your flesh and blood
sixteen dynasties playing with a reflection   seeking
a single opportunity limited by the burning of the dead
you hear   some empty stomach echoes in all directions
vomiting tradition

A ZÜRICH SWAN

as he says   happiness takes the form of a dirge
hanging on to a beauty it doesn't know
the dancing waters   have feigned sleep for seven hundred years
shooting a hurried glance at the person on the bridge's arch
 as she says   if you can't retrieve it then chew it bit by bit
another snowstorm plunging into the armpit
orange-red beaks stretch one by one toward a familiar-seeming shore
the ardour of the flesh   craves discarding

a twitching quill pen   had it signed more deathbeds
would still be singular   as he said when he stood on the water
as she   recognising in its reflections the only coldly overlapped swan
flapping broken wings on the riverbed   says   sunlight is cud-chewed
the beauty of fingers lies in holding tightly on to obscurity
 leaking the blue of the inner self   a more dazzling setting for a silver chain
bent into its own blood-fouled ornament
confirming the great bird's frenzy   dirge-like serenity

群山变白

当山脊的轮廓线坠入一个名字
睡在他小屋里的一夜　云中有人走过
雪碎步抵达冷妹妹的海拔
梦中的眼睛更白
书中袅袅的晶体泄露一个遗嘱
遗下　一张木床边群山彻夜的工作
那件老乐器弹奏了又弹奏
他醒时的欢呼　他骨节内的刺痛

死者分享一场甜甜的内分泌
在天上亮晶晶争论　谁更象疯子
或处女　肺里输出沙沙响的钙
弄脏的枕头上洒满他的远眺
一个令岩石越无知越夺目的现在
木楼梯冻脆了　才承认妹妹的
篡改　他的脸一夜倒挂下悬崖
正探进窗子要一付墨镜去看早晨

仍

仍是回文诗　街上布满说谎的孩子
仍在世界薄薄的荷叶边上
云啃着拇指的小橡皮
不一样的仍　仍有
一只茧　抱着情人的汗味象抱着钢琴曲
起舞　舞步里子宫要命地痉挛
仍听着电报声把往事深深吻成一件
私事

傍晚铸造的暴风雨的钢印
不停砸坏一个名字
桦树林的皮肤比旧衣服还旧
鸟声　自转着羞怯的新
仍暗中滑下孵出星星的热热轨道
月亮疼痛的好　街回肉色涨红的一分钟
孩子　交出藏在手里的死鸟
交出双翅深处没用的距离

THE MOUNTAINS TURN WHITE

as the outline of the ridge drops into a name
night sleeps in his little room   someone has walked over the clouds
snow tiptoes to reach the freezing sister's elevation
eyes are whiter in dreams
swaying crystals in book leak a testament
bequeathed   beside a wooden bed the mountains work all night
the old instrument has played and plays again
his cheer on waking   the stabbing pain in his joints

the dead share in a sweet secretion
glittering they debate in the sky   who is more like a madman
or a virgin   lungs export rustling calcium
the dirty pillow sprinkled with his distant gaze
a now that makes rock more ignorant the more it dazzles
wooden ladder frozen brittle   only now acknowledges sister's
distortion   his face hangs overnight on the cliff
stretches into the window wanting sunglasses to see the morning

STILL

still is a palindrome   street filled with lying children
still is on the thin edge of the lotus-leaf of the world
cloud nibbling a little eraser thumb
different kinds of still   there's still
a cocoon   embracing a lover's body odour like embracing a piano solo
dancing   womb in fatal convulsion in the dance-steps
still listening to the telegram's sound french-kissing the past into a
private matter

late afternoon casts the embossing stamp of the storm
endlessly smashing out a name
birchwood skin even older than old clothes
birdsong   spinning a bashful novelty
still in darkness slips down the blazing orbit that hatches stars
the pains of the moon good   carries one flesh-pink minute back in its beak
children   hand over the dead bird hidden in the hand
hand over the useless distance in the depth of the wings

185

她们

象牙白的微笑拎着她们
漫过街对面的屋顶
目光　一房间阳光继续上妆
灌溉书桌上一株虎皮兰的母性
天空双双嵌进镜框　旧照中
一场疾病刷新她们共同的美
一道瀑布似的时差轻拍骨肉
四季鱼贯而入梦中骗人的恒温

玻璃天堂来了　脸　别处茫茫的销魂
玻璃篱笆的家编进她们死后的周岁
旧食谱拎着星球上所有的墙
成群鸽子被一个埋在小公园里的爱牵引
呼啸而下　继续包扎
底片开始于生前的分娩
嗅着孩子的血找到每一条地平线
她们来了　解下围巾　从茶杯里凝视陌生人

影戏

痛苦就象美　以自身为目的
墙是一只猫行走的舞台
而舞　是一场第三人称的大红大绿
深处有只手抛着落日　影子间
相爱的器官　攥紧了蝙蝠的尖叫
相弃　黄昏翩翩于一付掌心的肉垫上
猫眼中每一刹那都正纵身一跃
故乡　被剪裁

逗留于一朵刺青
一个角色被无限剥制成戏剧
灯光剥制着晚霞　捕捉侧过身子的现实
影子们褴褛地披着人格
每天缝合一场大笑　深处
那只杀手在响应　猫爪下
所有落日舔到自己的无血
相挟而入鼓掌的黑　抱着礼物睡去

186

THEM (feminine plural)

ivory-white smiles carrying them
flood the roofs across the street
gaze   a roomful of sunlight continues to put on make-up
maternally watering the mother-in-law's tongue on the desk
the paired sky is inserted in a mirror   a pair of hands fluttering
a sickness refreshes the beauty they share
refreshes an old photo   a waterfall pats flesh and blood like a time difference
seasons in single file enter the constant temperature of cheating dreams

glass heaven has come   faces   vast vague ecstasy elsewhere
a house with glass fences is woven into their post-mortem years
an old recipe carrying every wall on the planet
flocks of doves towed by a love buried in the little park
whistling down   continue packing
the negative film begins with nativity before birth
sniffing the child's blood to find every horizon
they have come   taken off scarves   stared from teacups at strangers

SHADOW PLAY

pain is like beauty   with the self as the aim
the wall is an arena for a walking cat
and the dance   is third-person kitschy red & green
backstage a hand is lowering the setting sun   between the shadows
organs in love   hold the bat-squeaks tight
breaking up   dusk dances on the fleshy mat of a palm
in the cat's eye each instant is leaping
skin   bearing the weight of the cut-out hometown

captured in the tattoo's bud
a role is endlessly skinned into theatre
lamplight skinning the gloaming   catching reality turn itself half over
shadows raggedly wear personalities
laugh the laugh sewn together daily   backstage
the murderous hand responds   under the cat's claw
all setting suns lapping their own bloodlessness
supporting each other into the blackness of applause, asleep cuddling gifts

父亲的青花

一小罐深夜　窗外一千条国界怀着他
老年的天空继续窑变
继续整理这盆花草　灯光
上釉的手　炼制一场蓝色的咳嗽
他在肉里刺绣后代们易碎的白
千百次转身　一间小屋的
蛇腹吞下人生最长的直径
他通霄的醒　象全世界在梦呓

醒着不看人类　甚至不等
一杯黑暗的茶　四壁柔软地滑上去
小铁桌坠入粘满毒液的甬道
又一只烧红的圆封存
他的书　无人阅读时敛紧双翅
第几个开了又谢的把玩的七十岁
用刮不掉的花瓣惊动一件器皿
睡下　再露出白昼的胎记

入口

嗅着河的鼻子　簇新的指南针
街头流淌晚会金黄色的蜜
阳光一半埋在过去　却又是九点钟
魔术师裹紧自己象座秋风中的岛
翻开门牌　邮差褪掉点点鹦鹉绿
云靠拢梳妆台　珍珠粉和咖啡
汇成窗帘后面浑浊的下游
魔术师打开箱子　说变就变

桥象塑料宝石颗颗五光十色
星期日　象采访者塞入行人嘴里的字
流浪汉缠在街心公园的线轴上
阳台系着丝带　满满一只礼品盒
的血　被魔术师袖起
一件深蓝大氅呼拉拉撒出漫天落叶
波浪的五指捏住铸铁码头　一抖
漩涡中旋下去漫步的锈蚀的伦敦

FATHER'S BLUE & WHITE PORCELAIN

a small jar of night   a thousand frontiers carrying him
the sky of old age continues the firing in the kiln
continues arranging this pot plant   lamplight
a glazed hand   refines a blue cough
in his flesh he embroiders the fragile whiteness of posterity
turns around a thousand times   the little
room a snake's stomach swallows the longest diameter of life
his night-long waking   like the sleep-talk of the whole world

awake and not looking at humans   not even waiting for
a cup of darkness tea   four walls softly slide up
a small iron table sinks in to a venom-coated shaft
another red-hot circle sealing
his book   its unread wings tightly closed
how many bloomings and fadings of seventieth birthdays have been fondled
startling a container with petals that cannot be rubbed away
lying down   revealing again the birthmark of day

ENTRANCE

sniffing the river's nose   brand-new compass needle
the street flows with a party of golden honey
sunlight half-buried in the past   and it's nine o'clock again
a magician ties himself up like an island in the autumn breeze
turning house numbers over   the postman sheds drops of parrot green
clouds press in on the dressing table   powdered pearl and coffee
turbidly converging behind the curtains downstream
the magician opens the box   it changes at his word

bridge like radiantly bright plastic gemstones
sunday   like a word stuffed into a passer-by's mouth by the interviewer
a tramp entangled in the spool of the little park at the junction
balcony wearing a silk sash   a gift box
full of blood   palmed by the magician
a great deep blue mantle snaps open and spills a sky full of fallen leaves
the waves' fingers pinch a cast-iron dock   give it a shake
in the eddy a strolling rust-eaten downward-whirling London

你身上的园子

贴近去嗅那两只冻得肉色青紫的
浆果　才有股十二月的味儿
贴紧泥泞草叶上最初的白霜
几乎看见你的子宫
在分娩雪花
一上午的树枝　拍落满地金黄色的污点
你用一堵红砖墙向天空不停倾泻
那只小松鼠　漏出画框的灰烬

胎儿探出头　深及这间卧室
乌云象睡衣甩到钉子上　活
签署窗口右下角一个模糊的日期
名字冷冷调着一小瓶指甲油
阴唇懒洋洋噘起　说又一年已收拾好
一只公猫躺进你空出的那片蓝
两场雪吓人的间歇
鸟嘴上奔跑的诗　无非着了魔的字

复述的空间

空不能被说两次　犹如风暴只刮一次
你城市里的大雪忙着堆起玻璃渣
星空图书馆正注册我们的双脚
你的脸藏进火车站　月台
月光般皎洁　绿色灯罩压低一道远方的眉毛
一滴呆呆愣在窗外的雨细细摸着距离
我们彼此翻开　风中
梧桐叶死死抓住枯干的五指

等待的箴言浇铸你屋顶上的海鸥
我们的皮肤洗出了药香
酷爱分泌的琴　还陷进一张珊瑚床
日子抱紧湿淋淋的你
地下一把鲜红的树冠向内撑开
我们的肉伞罩住两座阳台
谁也看不见　情人骑着雪橇追上悬崖
风暴只刮一次　而一次已用尽百年

THE GARDEN ON YOU

only if you move closer and smell the flesh of those two frozen bruise-purple
berries   will there be the smell of December
huddle close into the first white frost on the muddy blades of grass
almost seeing your womb
giving birth to snowflakes
a whole morning of branches   spreading golden stains over the ground
you use a red brick wall to pour endlessly toward the sky
that little squirrel   ashes leaking from picture-frames

an embryo pops out its head   as deep as this bedroom
dark clouds like pyjamas flung on a nail   live
signing a blurry date in the bottom right corner of the window
name coldly stirring a small bottle of nail varnish
labia languidly pouting   saying 'another year tidied up'
a tomcat lying into the blue you emptied
intermission between two scary snowstorms
the rushing poem on the bird's beak   no more than words bewitched

RETOLD SPACE

void can't be told twice   as a storm blows only once
you city snow busily heaping up shards of glass
library of the night sky enrolling our feet
your face hidden in the railway station   platform
pale and pure as moonlight   green lampshade pushes down a distant eyebrow
outside the window a stupefied raindrop finely touching distance
we open each other out   in the wind
leaves of the parasol tree firmly grip five withered fingers

a waiting exhortation moulds the seagulls on your rooftop
our washed skin smells of medicine
adoring the secreting string instrument   fallen into a bed of coral
the days tightly hold a soaking you
on the ground a bright red tree-crown opens inward
the umbrella of our flesh covers two balconies
no-one can see   the lover on the sledge rushing up the cliff
a storm blows only once   but once exhausts a century

余下的时间

发炎的充血的上腭是一幅天顶画
病人　还有什么被余下
除了眺望再生一次的病那条地平线
现在的小小石龛变得更小时
回声等待一架管风琴
黄昏　音符里沉甸甸发育着黄金
一只深陷进象牙的鸟呼叫别处
一个子宫内剖出的寒冷在到处

床边整片风景推不动一盏烛火之处
情人嘴里摇荡着另一半悬梯
总象还将到来的　目的
总是肉里一座盲目守住余音的钟楼
诗人　最好的背叛是听完这支安魂曲
夜空越晚越敲响一块变色的大理石
远远辉映余下的疼
等　到　关掉这世界

THE TIME THAT'S LEFT

the bright red inflamed palate is a painting of the zenith
the patient   what is left of him
apart from scanning the horizon of the disease caught again
as the tiny stone niche of now becomes smaller
an echo awaiting a pipe organ
twilight   gold growing heavily in the notes
a bird sunk deep in ivory calls out for elsewhere
a coldness sliced from the womb is everywhere

where the entire bedside scene can't push a candle flame over
swinging the other half of the hanging ladder in a lover's mouth
always like the yet to arrive   aim
is always a bell tower in the flesh blindly guarding lingering sound
the poet   the best betrayal is to listen to this requiem complete
the later the night the louder the night sky rings chameleon marble
distantly reflecting pain that's left
waiting   to   switch off this world

艳诗

5. *from* Dark Blue Poems

我们做爱的小屋（代序）

这隐匿深处的房间只为你留着
为一对抱紧我的细细的胳膊留着
暗绿色的花袍子　感到一种软
来自轻轻磨擦的乳房　在把玩
一株肉质植物里索索发抖的时间
你的裸体　只为我的目光留着

一次插到底　二十年就成了漩涡
一次　整个背麻了　电击的血脉
让到处　哪怕山巅　渗出室内的幽暗
把器官暴露在阳光下　你要的满
非得含着宇宙那堆雪　才够满
二十年的凸透镜中我们更贪婪地做

总能更精美的　宛如咀嚼的
茎深深陷入一个处境　哦你又在收缩
白白浓浓的定影液冲洗一张底片
我们家的暗室　暗转大海的蓝
受不了时　二十年混淆两千年
数着暴风雨　细腰抖断了热热尿了

热流　最怕冷却的　疯至从未冷却的
娃娃们成群飞回你那只鸟窝
阴道吸住我一瞬　世界已换了又换
再搂紧些　当经纬线即来复线
四条腿钩住恰似板机的那一点
再射　爱刷新肉体　齐根擎着金荷

PROLOGUE — THE LITTLE ROOM WHERE WE MAKE LOVE

only for you this deep hidden room is kept
for a pair of slender arms to hold me tight it's kept
dark green fi gured gown   a kind of soft feeling
a lightly rubbed breast   fondling
time inside the fleshy plant's solitary trembling
your flesh   only for my eyes is kept

once it's stuck right in   whirlpool twenty years becoming
once   back numb all over   veins electric shocking
everywhere   even on the hilltop the room's dimness is inundated
exposing organs to the sunlight   by what you want sated
got to take the cosmic snow pile in your mouth   enough to be sated
in the twenty-year magnifying glass we're more greedily fucking

what can always be finer   seems to be chewing
root deeply penetrating the predicament   again you're contracting
thick white fi xing solution washes a negative out
our house's darkroom   blacks the blue of the ocean out
when it's too good to bear   twenty years mixed in two thousand
                                                    fading out
counting storms   slim waist shaken apart in hot pissing

hot flow   most afraid of the cool   so crazy it can never get cool
fl ying back to your bird's nest babies in flocks forgather
vagina inhales me for an instant   world changed and again changing
hugs tighter   longitude and latitude turn into rifl ing
four legs hooked together like a trigger preparing
to shoot again   love to renew flesh   holding up a golden lotus root

承德行宫

宫女们羞答答穿上朕杜撰的裤子了
她们袒露的阴部　令锦缎失色
朕的眼中再没有湖山　画舫回廊
帝国呢　小于一个香的三角形缺口
毛间翘起一点红　哦朕的杰作

随便哪儿　只要鹿血在心里弹跳
只要朕又硬了　又想猛插入一声惊叫
玉碗粉碎　朕命你满捧另一杯茶
雪水烹的　水声潺潺象个早死的先兆
天子倒悬于天空下　饮　在聚焦

这个朕想废就废掉的一生
妩媚啊　她们倒下扒开自己的样子
也把朕剥光了　肉收紧一座后宫
朕就拔不出来了　精液热热地一涌
行云布雨　沿着最美的毁灭的捷径

弯刀

　　　　　　苏丹的帝国动摇了
你身上每根会跳舞的线条
都被一道寒光领向
指尖与刀尖互相戳疼的交点

血五颜六色
宝石伏在脚踝上象串水蛭
一弯湿漉漉的刃分泌着亮度

　　　　　　苏丹的目光被砍伤
纱衫下你那道要命的缝
挑着两个半圆　两条鹿腿　两片唇
世界就从这儿一点点裂开

IMPERIAL PALACE AT JEHOL

bashfully the palace girls put on Our invented trousers
their privates exposed   till brocade loses its colours
in Our eyes no more lakes and hills   painted junks   curving corridors
empire   less than the triangle's scented crease
a point of pink among the hair   oh Our masterpiece

anywhere at all   only for stag's blood in Our heart springing
only for Us to be hard again   and a cry of surprise fiercely penetrating
jade bowl shattered   We command you to serve another cup of tea
made with melted snow   water gurgling like an omen dying early
Son of Heaven suspended from the sky   drinking   focuses us fairly

this life We could throw away if We wanted to
how entrancing!   The way they fall as if brushing themselves aside
and strip Us bare too   their meat tightens in the golden seraglio
so We can't pull out   a hot spurt of come   in action
spreading wind and water   on the loveliest shortcut to destruction

SCIMITAR

                    the sultan's empire totters
every line of your body that can dance
is led by the cold gleam of blades
finger-end and sword-point each painfully stabbing the other

blood comes in many colours
a jewel lies on the ankle like a spitted leech
a wet arc secretes brightness as it flexes

                    the sultan's sight is wounded
below a gauzy caftan your killing crack
lifts two hemispheres   two deer legs   two lips
from here the world splits open little by little

窗外的雪地

准有人　谁呢　精心修剪过你的乳头
拨弄一下　那片白就变尖了
含进嘴里　那冷就鼓胀成荷花
舌头绕着玩早晨最红艳的一朵
准有光在掐它　捏紧它

勒着吊起　一个看不见的高度
俯在你身上　谁呀　推窗
就打开臆想　或甜　或咸　或腥
世界驾着横冲直撞的雪橇
不吝惜又一夜处女的嫩

不停　赠给你
一个泥泞飞溅的不知谁的自我
象阳光掏钻的小脏窟窿那么黑
蓝色倒映的裸河　枕着一块肉动了
腿下又湿又亮　你的蜜　融了

SNOWY GROUND BELOW THE WINDOW

there's definitely someone   who   carefully pruned your nipple
drew out   that white sharpened slice
taken into the mouth   that cold ballooned into a lotus
tongue circles as it plays with morning's reddest flower
there's definitely light pinching it   choking it

tying it and hanging it up   an invisible height
bending over your body   who pushed the window
to open a wild dream   sweet   or salty   or rank
the world riding a sledge that's running amok
never stinting the tenderness of virgins of another night

endlessly   giving to you
a sloppily splashed ego   who knows whose
black as the dirty little hole bored out by the sunshine
naked river reflecting blue   pillowing a piece of meat as it moves
wet and bright below the thigh   your honey   melting

紫郁金宫：慢板的一夜

后宫里的一夜总有月光　玉阶和珠帘
却都是想象的　一束花衬着壁纸的蓝
想象　妃子的紫衣下一堆雪在坍塌
急急等待被占用的雪　用结晶慢慢
转身　每分钟向内卷曲着慢慢舞蹈
一束郁金香璀璨的衰败脱下一场自恋
一种紫色的耳语　必须喘息着说
只对那人说　当他重重碾压着花瓣
一滴紫色的奶　像妃子急急等待被吸尽的
想着　全世界就涌进一根滚烫的脉管

后宫里的火　总有舌头百般的顽皮
被修剪的尖　舔到皮肤的空　午夜之绿
绿如片片堆叠在妃子脚踝处的叶子
那人的宠爱　一场来自所有方向的沐浴
浇淋他的花　乳头的紫玉小碗斟满了
报复一个时间　大海沉积在色素里
一束郁金香一夜从女高音滑入女中音
今夜　霸道之美对称着流逝的诗意
妃子只为那人保存的幽香　只交给他把玩
紫色的慢慢粉碎　丝光停不住时

后宫里总有闪烁成一个蕊的磷光
一根针指挥着　肉体四季被演奏的欲望
一种镂空的剪裁　镂空至妃子的生死
壁纸蓝蓝如一次缝合所有伤痛的狂想
只一次　花影中日子咬下的牙印
就无限发暗　这夜色无限鲜嫩　刺绣到身上
原初那次　紫　像滴慢慢洇开的奶
慢慢被宇宙吸收　纵容那人的黄　那么黄
凝视中赐给妃子一个黑尽的语法
当花瓶像个词圆圆贴着手掌

A NIGHT IN THE PURPLE TULIP PALACE (ADAGIO)

In this seraglio night always consists of   moonlight, jade steps and a
                                        curtain of pearls
all imaginary   a bunch of flowers against blue wallpaper
imagine   caving in under the concubine's clothes a mound of snow
snow waiting impatiently to be possessed its crystalline body slowly
turning   constantly curling in on itself in a slow dance
a bunch of tulips divesting itself of the love of self as it brightly declines
a kind of purple whisper which must be spoken breathily
addressing only him as he crushes the petals heavily
a drop of purple milk   like a concubine impatiently waiting to be sucked
concentrating   the entire world into one burning duct

In this seraglio   fire always has the rude playfulness of tongues
a pointed tip   licks the emptiness of skin   midnight's cling
green like leaves gathered at the concubine's ankles
his preference for her   a shower coming from every angle
watering the flower the little purple bowl of her nipple fills
in revenge against time   the pigment holds ocean's deepest spoils
a bunch of tulips slips in a single night from soprano to mezzo
tonight   tyrannous beauty is balanced by this aesthetic of erosion
this evasive scent which the concubine keeps for him alone   and only
                                        lets him savour
when the silky light can't stop   purple very gently splays open

In this seraglio there's always this dead bone phosphor light becoming
                                        a pistil's gleam
conducting the body's desire   to be played for all four seasons
carving out this hole cut through   the concubine's sculpted days
the wallpaper is blue like a crazy mind sewing up all past pains
only once   the hours' bitemarks into each flower
darken endlessly   the night is stitched onto flesh   endlessly fresh
                                        and tender
once in the beginning   purple   gradually spread like a drop of milk
slowly absorbed by the universe   which sees his lasciviousness   and winks
by staring he bestows on the concubine a totally dark grammar
the vase is like a word resting between the hands

Translated by W.N.Herbert and Yang Lian

SAILOR'S HOME

1. 春光·河谷

这一刻无限大　阳光裸出的身子那么大
裸着　一篷金色茸毛紧紧挤着
我们的头埋进去　河谷磨擦脸颊

这一刻　躺在怀里的是个春天的轮廓
轮到你了　闭上眼也觉得群山在下面
鸟鸣令子宫粉红幸福地收缩

风不动　五道血痕也追着五枚指尖
追上一条被你藏在羞涩里的缝
又香又软　推着绿绿的两岸

我们就看见　下次呼吸没有风景
河谷弯进光　光速在每滴水珠里崩溃
我们知道　令世界亮得晕眩的命

完成于一刹那　这一刻的心醉
亲吻这一刻的毁灭　抱紧是一朵花
抖着　勃起着　发烫的一点　就象蕊

2. LYN BEACH

海浪也一直在寻找　用风暴寻找
海把尖尖挺起的乳头递到你嘴里
童年　象绷紧的帆绳那样嘶叫

象排油漆斑驳的小房子　残破倾圮
却把一只耳朵的珍珠贝留在窗台上
涛声把小名舔剩银白的骸骨时

水平线忍着呻吟　水中抽出紫丁香
涨潮就在长大　一张从未压皱的床单
叫你怕　你要又一个四月被弄脏

SAILOR'S HOME

1 SPRING SCENE – RIVER VALLEY

this infinitely big moment   exposed by sunlight so big, this body
exposing   a mat of tightly-clustered golden down
our heads are buried in it   rubbing our cheeks a river valley

this moment   what lies embraced is the shape of spring
lined up for you   eyes closed you feel the hills are below
birdsong making your womb contract with pink blessing

wind stilled   bloodstains chasing the end of each finger
catching the crack you hide within your shyness
soft and fragrant   pushing the green banks of the river

so we see   next breath there's no scenery
river valley bends into light   lightspeed crumbling within each drop
of water
we know   the destiny that makes the world bright and dizzy

complete in an instant   this enchantment
kiss the destruction of the moment   the tight hug is the flower
trembling   erect   burning   point like a pistil or stamen

2 LYN BEACH

waves have been searching all along   storm searching
sea puts a sharp standing nipple in your mouth
childhood   like an overstretched halyard squealing

like a little room mottled with exuded paint   destroyed and dilapidated
leaving the pearl shell of an ear on the windowsill
when surf licks your nickname what's left is a skeleton, silver-white,
articulated

horizon surrers its groans   lilac from water pulled
so the tide is growing up   a never wrinkled bedsheet
makes you afraid   you want another April polluted

海滩的女性　无论怎样挪远
都有一条鱼鲜嫩的腹部　好继续学习疼
你长长的双腿盘紧这个傍晚

湿的拉力　一股拼命回头看的激情
用尽了海　肉盛满一罐哭声来到
一个黑到底的形式　才配追上你的诞生

3. 岸

水波粼粼作曲　不远处一架死钢琴
在潮汐中响着　死水手精心修剪的五指
摇曳　满房间白珊瑚和康乃馨

满含最后一瞥的性感　一盏烛火透视
性交的肉体中一个岸透明的结构
我们彼此是锚　彼此是锚地

蓝色动荡的家　一块皮肤就是港口
我们嵌着的缺口　炫耀大海空出的方向
死船长冷冰冰指挥一场演奏

音乐会就夹在我们大腿间　那流淌
一股血味儿　血淋淋挥舞器官的旗语
那茎指着说　没别的地方

你能去　你该去　墙上的死镜框里
一头蒙着蓝色条纹的兽慢慢逡巡
岸　记住最后一瞥　那一瞥无终无始

4. "水手之家"

一行字刻在墙上　不停出海的字
把孩子们变老了　不停疯长的蓝色花草
听小小的白眼珠在防波堤上哭泣

the beach's female sex   surely somehow far away shifting
with the delicate belly of a fish   to go on learning pain
your long legs twist hard around this gloaming

the pull of the wet   a desperate passion to turn and survey
has used up the sea   flesh fills a pot of sobs to arrive at
a form black all through   then it deserves to catch your birthday

3 SHORE

the waves' crystal composing   dead piano at an interval
in the sounding of the tides   dead sailor's carefully trimmed fingers
swaying   a room full of carnations and white coral

filled with the sexiness of a final stare   candle flame's x-ray visage
shore a transparent structure in the flesh of lovemaking
we are each other's anchor   we are each other's anchorage

shaky blue house   skin is the harbour
the crack inlaid in us   shows off the direction where the ocean empties
the dead captain icily conducts the overture

the concert is squeezed between our thighs   the flow
a whiff of blood   semaphore that waves bloody organs
the root says as it points   no other place to go

you can go   you should go   in the dead mirror-frame on the panelling
the beast that covers over blue clauses slowly withdraws
shore   remember the last stare   stare with no end or beginning

4 SAILOR'S HOME

a line of words carved on the wall   words endlessly sailing
making children old   endlessly overgrown blue plants
on the breakwaters hear white eyeballs weeping

父亲的精液是一个异国　被一道
盛满明媚早晨的裂缝隔开
母亲　躲进海鸥茫然的啼叫

分别就再次分娩　把这团血肉遗下来
又一排小小的白浪头把远方打得更远
孩子们否认海那边有个世界

不停构思着　把阳光变黑的血缘
把岸变得狂暴　把被抛弃当作一件作品
那时间表上永不到来的时间

永远卡在　即将挤出血腥隘口的一瞬
母亲哭嚎　父亲肿胀的阴囊低垂
如星座　蠕动　孩子否认不了的命运

5. 午睡的海图

光在窗外倾泄　漂过床头的白色水母
累了　半透明的室内象只半闭的眼帘
鱼类五彩的尾巴围着蜡烛

她睡在就象死在海底卵石间
死了　还梦见一丛被摆布的黑色海草
肉体那么无知　肉体持续下潜

丝丝痒的脚趾　触到嘴唇软软的珊瑚礁
化了　舌头追赶一阵脚踝上的麻
嘶嘶向里窜　一封拍往全身的电报

海香喷喷捻着一朵空间的茶花
开了　魔鬼揉弄酷似蚌肉的一小只
比她还象动物　越抽搐越湿滑

亮晶晶挣脱妄想捏拢的手指
逃了　镜子张望中　镜子还在画出
颓废的宋朝的鹤侧着身子

father's semen is a foreign land   separated by
the crack filled with radiant morning sunlight
mother   hides in the seagull's blank cry

once more separation gives birth   abandons this piece of vellum
another row of thin white waves beating far into farther
children deny that beyond the sea there is another realm

endlessly plotting   sunshine-blackening ancestry
maddening the shore   turning being forsaken into a work of art
the time that never comes is in the directory

forever blocked   at the instant that will squeeze through the bloody
                                                    chimney
mother wails   father's swollen dropped scrotum hangs down
like a constellation   wriggling   children's undeniable destiny

5 CHART OF A NAP

light floods out beyond the window   white jellyfish floating by the
                                                    bed-head
tired   semi-transparent interior like a half-closed eye
dancing multi-coloured fish tailsaround the candle spread

among sea floor pebbles her sleep imitates dying
dead   still dreaming a thicket of black sea weed under orders
as ignorant as a body   a body that just goes on diving

toe's tiny itches   a soft coral reef of lips gently collide
melted   tongues chase anaesthesia on the ankles
a telegram sent to the whole body   fizzing flees inside

sea odoriferously twists a camellia of space
opened   demon rubs and plays with a small clam-like thing
more like an animal than like her   the more it skids, the more it will pulse

glistening shakes off the pinching fingers of hope that's vain
escaped   in the mirror's distant gaze   mirror still painting
lying on its side a decadent Song dynasty crane

6. 午睡的海图

海面上一百万个玫瑰园泛起嫣红
床上　颈窝是精雕细刻的一小朵
别碰那乳头　让她去做梦

让两个尖　在梦中接受一种熏香的颜色
让一下午把滴滴溢出的奶噙在嘴里
此刻搂在胸前的　都是出海的

睡着　一座城市也在漂移
一双放肆的脚践踏波浪的鳞状台阶
迎向耀眼灾难的　总是一次深呼吸

满屋冉冉上升着气泡
满屋弯曲的动作　擦过被耳语提前的夜
不问也知道　小憩　正变成性交

人造的一夜中合上眼就有想要的明月
人　是块礁石收藏着结束的阴影
为抛弃存在而一股股倾泄

7. 水晶宫

时代的丑陋鱼群隔着窗户一片死寂
它们的目光　扎穿石棺里那些年
翻找一枚红艳的被磨烂的阴蒂

死死纠缠的躯体上　两个极端
都插着　舌头与茎都涨成一大块水晶
塞得更满时　顶到藏得更深的终点

死死纠缠的躯体　不再回顾才透明
死过上千次的大海的卵巢
猛吸一口血　不在乎失去才怕人的硬

210

6 CHART OF A NAP

on the sea's surface a million flaming red rose gardens are drifting
on the bed   the hollow of the throat is a little precisely carved one
don't knock that nipple   let her go dreaming

let two tips   in dreams the perfumed colour of smoke inhale
let an afternoon hold in its mouth milk seeping out drop by drop
what this instant hugs to its breast   has all set sail

sleeping   this city too is floating off
on the scaly steps of the surf two feet run wild
what's facing dazzling disaster   is always one deep breath

the room is filled with bubbles imperceptibly rising
the flexing everywhere in the room   grazes the whisper-brought night
know without asking   a little rest   is turning into screwing

in man-made night you see the bright moon when your eyes close
man   is a reef collecting shadows of endings
pouring out in a flood to throw away existence

7 CRYSTAL PALACE

a window separates from deathly stillness the ugly shoals of this time
their visions   stabbing through the years in the stone sarcophagus
rummaging for a bright red clitoris rubbed into slime

on tightly tangled bodies   doubly extreme
both inserted   both tongue and root swollen into one huge crystal
stuffed even fuller   it butts against the more deeply hidden demesne

tightly tangled bodies   only transparent if they never look back again
ovary of the ocean that thousands of times has died
violently exhales a mouthful of blood   only scarily hard if it lives
                                                                    with losing

找到你　封存的初夜象一张初稿
黑暗象一座窗台　又摆出那盆绣球花
只让我看见　你的美已准备好

崩溃　交配的星空停进第一场大爆炸
一大团喷出的雪白没有过去
石头里走投无路的水　才抵达

8. 复数

这个现在的复数　蓝的复数
水手漂白的身影漂浮在每道波峰上
折射成无从等待的　溺死是复数

仍自一块棱形切下水平线的　是光
仍一再改写住址的　是总嚷着还要的海
又一具射精后的尸骸被啐到石凳上

空得象海哩　绿色家俱摆满悬崖
满是时差的房间睁开有对羊眼的早晨
谁沦为无从等待的　自己不得不等待

一把水手片片削落果肉的利刃
一次都不在　却被咀嚼了无数次
一个我都不剩　才毁灭成我们

粉碎　定居在狠狠砸下的涛声里
甚至停止不了渴望一个孤独腐烂的单数
守着　摔在远方礁石上的名字

9. 绞架上的苹果

你用整整一年想像插进自己里面的核
一根旋转的轴　一种你想否认的力
否认不了　秋天是把绞杀的文火

finding you   sealed first night like a page first drafted
darkness like a windowsill   displays again a pot of hydrangeas
only let me see   your beauty all ready crafted

collapse   starry sky of sex stopping in the first big bang
big ball of spat-out snow white has no past
water helplessly locked in stone   has only now come along

8 PLURAL

the plural of now   plural is blue
bleached shadows of sailors floating on the crests of every wave
refracted into what can't be awaited   drowning is plural too

what still cuts the horizon from the prism   is radiance
what still endlessly re-writes addresses   is the sea yelling for more
another post-coital skeleton spat out on a stone bench

it's empty as nautical miles   green furniture set out across the precipice
the room holding all time differences opens the sheep eyes of morning
who sinks into what can't be awaited   self has to wait for this

sharp blade for sailors to peel off fruit flesh in slices
doesn't once exist   though chewed times without number
not an I is left   destroyed only then to become us

shatter   domiciled in the heartless pounding surf
can't even stop longing for a lonely rotting singular
watching   a name flung on the distant reef

9 APPLE ON THE GALLOWS

you take all year to imagine inserting the kernel stuck inside you
a revolving axle   a kind of force you want to deny
can't deny   autumn is a slow fire for death and hanging too

一个碧蓝的拎着你在空中晃的逻辑
离地几米高　涨红的果肉抱着核摩擦时
风摸你　此刻谁想摸就摸你

冷钉进内心　甜才格外放肆
腐烂有个把柄　攥住就嗅到性的腥香
你把自己挂上一枚黄金的倒刺

离世界几米高　交给最粗暴的光
磨快尖利的鸟嘴　知道啄哪儿更为致命
啄她　碎肉零落　枝头震荡

一双第一天已深深看进肉里的眼睛
用必死的诗意　让你想像一次猛烈的活
带着孤零零悬挂的被引爆的表情

10. 圣丁香之海

这一刻无限大　花　迸开在人的尽头
激动中　天空的紫色　海的白色
驶出我们身上每处奋张的港口

水里满是心跳　水的厄运是一生去触摸
一根埋在肉中绷直抽动的管子
一个不停拧紧蓓蕾乳头的四月

输送　灿烂皮肤下我们的无知
紫色和白色　都被体内的黑暗驱赶到空中
漫无目的　以急急奔赴一次自焚为目的

这一刻　碎裂的生殖器鲜艳就是目送
春天的香味就象烟味　一把把绸伞撑开
末日抵进嘴里　惊叫都学着鸟鸣

肉体的形象是不够的　最终需要一滴泪
出走到花园里　星际嫩嫩漂流
每阵风吹走大海

indigo logic that lifts you swaying in space
metres above the ground   when flushed fruits hold their kernels and rub
wind touches you   whoever wants to can touch you in this place

cold nails your inner being   sweet limitless only then for yourself
rot has a handle   clutching and smelling the fishy fragrance of sex
on a golden barb you hang yourself

metres above the world   given over to the crudest brilliance
beak that sharpens its point   knows where pecking is more mortal
pecks her   broken flesh withered   vibrating branch

two eyes that saw deep into the flesh on that first day
take the poetic of necessary death   to make you imagine one fierce life
a detonated facial expression hanging and lonely

10 HOLY LILAC SEA

this instant is infinitely large   flowers   spurt at humans' end
in excitation   purple of the sky   white of the sea
drive out of the harbours on our flesh forced and opened

water is full of heartbeats   water's bad luck is life-long touch
the stiff twitching tube buried in the flesh
April endlessly twisting nipple buds in its clutch

shipped   our ignorance beneath splendid skin
purple and white   expelled into the sky by the body's own dark
random   aiming for the hasty rush to self-immolation

this instant   the shine of shattered sex organs is a long look of goodbye
spring's perfume like smoke's smell   silken parasols opening one by one
final day lowered into our mouth   all your cries learning from a bird's cry

only the body's image isn't enough   at last a tear drop has fallen
leaving for the garden   stars tenderly drifting
each breath of wind blowing away the ocean

Lightning Source UK Ltd.
Milton Keynes UK
UKOW02f1909280217
295586UK00001B/181/P